Eliminate the Losers

A TESTED METHOD FOR SUCCESSFUL HANDICAPPING

BOB McKNIGHT

1978 EDITION

Published by
Melvin Powers
WILSHIRE BOOK COMPANY
12015 Sherman Road
No. Hollywood, California 91605
Telephone: (213) 875-1711

Second paperbound printing, 1972

ISBN 0-87980-319-3

Published by arrangement with Citadel Press
(a subsidiary of Lyle Stuart, Inc.)

Printed by

HAL LEIGHTON PRINTING CO.
P.O. Box 1231
Beverly Hills, California 90213
Telephone: (213) 983-1105

Contents

CHAPTER ONE   *Condition*

I wonder how many of you California racing fans recall the Del Mar racing plant of a dozen or so years ago, which used to get the afternoon's activities under way with a recording by Bing Crosby, who at that time owned a piece of the establishment? The words to the song, as they oozed by Der Bingle's larynx, went something like this: "There's a smile on every face, and a winner in every race, where the turf meets the surf at Del Mar."

That's what the man said—a winner in every race. And wouldn't it be something if we could prognosticate every one of them?

Actually, it would be ghastly—like getting tomorrow's results today. What could be more monotonous? Well, we won't worry about it. You and I—no matter how good we are at picking winners, or how good we think we are, which is something else again—will never get to the point where we can pick the winner in *every* race.

What we *can* do is correctly predetermine enough of them at sufficiently high mutuel payoffs so that our gross return will consistently exceed our investment. And that, fellers and gals, is nice work if you can get it.

And you *can* get it, depending on how much persistence,

beetle-browed study, and self-control you're willing to bring to the chore. The fact that you have picked up this tome and read this far already has you out of the gate and on the pace.

There is a reason for everything that happens in racing. If the favorite is beaten by a long shot, there is a reason. If the speed horse is beaten by a slower one, there is a reason. If the class horse is beaten by a cheapie, there is a reason.

Often it is the same reason—peak condition, or the loss of it. For this is the one factor that controls all others. The speed-burner will not be able to display or maintain his blazing speed if he is out of condition. The class horse will not be able to make his superiority felt if he is out of condition.

Condition, then, is the real gimmick in racing, and one of the hardest of all the factors to determine accurately at the time when it counts. *Today*. Now that the race is about to be contested.

When we consider that the racing secretary has done his level best to bring a band of horses together, each of which will have an equal chance to win, and that he has written his condition book weeks in advance of this race at a time when he was in no better position than you and I to gauge the actual physical fitness of each beastie today—now, with the race about to be run, it is evident that the final judgment of this vastly important factor has been left to the trainer—and to you and to me.

Since the trainer is so much closer to the picture than we, and is an expert at the business of bringing his horse to hand (trained to winning pitch), why not leave it up to him? Why need we worry about it at all? If his horse is off form, he'd have scratched him, wouldn't he?

No, not necessarily. Though many times I have had what for me figured to be a mortal cinch scratched, leaving me with an unplayable race. Though a trainer's reason for declaring a horse out of a race is rarely made public, in most cases we have to presume it was because the beastie came up with an ailment not foreseeable at the time he was entered.

To get a clearer picture of what goes on behind the scenes: A trainer places a certain one of his nags in training and observes him carefully through the weeks of training for signs that he is coming to hand. Guessing that the hide will be ready in two weeks, he consults the condition book, picks a race he considers suitable, and enters the horse.

Maybe the horse is ready on time. Maybe not. Or maybe he even comes to hand ahead of time and has already lost some of his moxie when the race is finally contested. In the latter case, the trainer is not going to waste many weeks of training. He is going to take a chance and hope his horse has enough edge left to do the job, or even get part of the purse. If, on the other hand, his horse has not quite come to hand when the race is scheduled, he will let him run, knowing he is not ready to win but expecting him to get his final tightening in this race so that he will be on edge to win his next start.

There is another, more intangible reason why trainers do not scratch. They get high on their own stock. After all, your puppy is much better than Joe Blow's, even though they're both out of the same litter. Well, trainers are human, too. So human, in fact, that they sometimes get the idea they've done a magnificent job of training, when at best it was only mediocre.

You still think we ought to leave this important decision entirely up to the trainer? I say "entirely" advisedly, for to a certain extent we have to trust him, unless we ourselves are good judges of condition and can go to the paddock before a race and determine for ourselves—simply by looking—whether or not the nag we plan to back is, or is not, up to par. Some people can. Others think they can. But I suspect that most of the cash customers who gang up around the paddock are hoping, by the close proximity, to get a hunch.

However, I used to have a housekeeper, a big rawboned ranch gal from out Wyoming way, who knew her horseflesh. Not thoroughbred horseflesh—but horses. To the best of my knowledge she had never been to a thoroughbred track before my wife and I took her one day.

She picked her horses on sight at the paddock. And she did all right, without so much as a glance at the past performances, where the nag's capabilities were set down for all to see and evaluate.

To give a practical example of what happens when we ignore present condition or trust the trainer in this highly important matter, we are going to take the highest speed horse in a full day's card, ignore condition, and see what happened. The fastest horse should get home free. Right?

We spear a *Daily Racing Form* at random, this in preference to the *Morning Telegraph* because the *Form* publishes an index of the best time each contestant had made at today's distance during the past couple of years. The *Telegraph* does not. Also, the *Telegraph* is published in New York, and though copies are flown hither and yon for the faithful, by far the majority of fans have only the *Form* available to them.

So this issue of the *Form* happens to be February 3, 1962. Flipping it open to the first set of past performances, we find ourselves at New Orleans, at the Fair Grounds track.

We simply take the fastest time in the Index without qualifying the horse as to present condition. For this test, we're leaving the condition factor entirely up to the trainer, (remember).

In the first race at the Fair Grounds, the fastest time listed in the Index was 1:10⅖ and the horse that made it was Luke's Charm. This is six-furlong time, of course, the distance of today's race.

Luke's Charm was beaten by Colonel O.O., a horse with much slower Index time, but whose present condition was obviously superior to Luke Charm's. (For the present, please take my word for that. Later we'll investigate any number of ways to determine condition so that you yourself will be able to do it accurately.)

In the second race, there were two horses with exactly the same Index speed. Austin Venn, with a bit the best of it on condition, won the race.

In the third race, we again have two horses tied for speed honors—made, you understand, at some time during the last couple of years. Neither of these hides could be said to be in or near peak condition. Neither one of them got any part of the money. The horse that won it, Be Diamond, was *obviously* the fastest one of this group *at this time* by virtue of his superior condition, as near as you and I could judge it from available figures in the past performances.

Do you think Be Diamond's trainer did not know he had a sharp horse going? Do you think the trainers of the other two did not know their horses were not at peak form?

There is more than one way of looking at this. If only the top-condition horse were allowed to run, there would be no race. No contest. And the trainers with horses not yet quite come to hand, or just over the peak, are always hopeful that the breaks may give them a purse. A traffic pattern could conceivably change the outcome. An error in judgment by the jockey on the condition horse could change the outcome. A spill could upset the applecart.

In this connection, we recall—way back yonder when there

were not such tight controls on racing—a hide whose name was Stickler, if memory serves us right. It should have been Stinkler, for this fugitive from the glue works could not outrun a fat lady. But his trainer was a persistent cuss, who also believed in the inevitability of racing miracles.

He entered his beastie in race after race after race, and there could be no question that Stinkler was a paragon of consistency. He always finished last.

Then one day, the miracle happened. The field, all but Stinkler, was tightly bunched going into the far turn. One of the nags ran up onto the heels of another, and the whole field piled up in a nasty spill. All but Stinkler, who was so far to the rear that his jockey had plenty of time to steer him clear of the pile-up. So he, at long last, went on to win, all by himself.

But to get back to our test case, here is the list of speed horses (without benefit or qualifying for present condition), and how they fared:

RACE	HORSE	WIN	PLACE	SHOW
1	Luke's Charm	$ ...	$6.80	$5.00
2	{ Paul I	...	...	...
	{ Austin Venn	9.40	5.20	3.60
3	{ Royal Beggar	...	...	...
	{ Double Disc	...	...	...
4	Tamboro	...	...	...
5	Coylind	5.40	3.60	3.00
6	Loil Roil	...	5.20	4.20
7	Big Patton	...	...	2.60
8	Little Atlas	...	...	...
9	Fortunate Isle	...	...	2.80

Not very exciting results, are they? But not surprising, either, considering that we left such an important factor as present condition out of our calculations. Or rather, left it up to the trainer who may have had something else in mind entirely. Like Stinkler's miracle. Or tightening his charge up for a winning effort in his *next* trip to the post. For it is a generally accepted fact along Shed Row that, once a certain point in the training program has been reached, nothing is quite so beneficial for putting on the winning edge as an actual race.

Now then, in order to give real meaning to the workout just presented, we must be able to make a comparison. How would the list, and the results, have been different if we *had* insisted on qualification by present condition?

For the sake of consistency (not of the Stinkler variety), we will again consider the top speed horse in the Index, but we will not list him for play unless we can satisfy ourselves as to his present condition. So, he must have raced fairly recently— say, within two weeks—and in that recent race he must have earned a speed within five lengths (one second, or five-fifths of a second) of his best time as shown in the Index.

Luke's Charm shows 1:10⅖ in the Index. Remember? In his last race—on January 31, just three days ago—his time for the same distance over a fast strip was 1:16. His last race was twenty-seven fifths (lengths) slower than his best race. Even if that last race tightened him, we have limited ourselves to a five-point differential, so we could not qualify Luke's Charm for play under these conditions, or, to be more exact, in his apparent condition.

In the second race, we will remember that both Paul I and Austin Venn, showed speeds of 1:11⅗ or I should say, we will remember that they both showed the same best speed of the field against which they are entered today.

Paul I raced last on January 16, which was eighteen days ago. And since he shows no work since then, we can give him no further consideration.

Austin Venn raced last on January 17, which was seventeen days ago. But he worked on January 25, which was only eight days ago, so let's check his speed in that last race since we can assume his racing edge has been kept sharp by recent work. This race was contested on a good (gd) track, which is some five points slower than a fast track. Thus, Austin Venn's 1:12⅘ is comparable to the 1:11⅗ he made on a fast strip for his best time. On this basis, Austin Venn can be qualified on condition.

In the third race, we again had tied speed contenders, Royal Beggar and Double Disc. The tied best time was 1:12⅕. Royal Beggar's last race was on January 20, which is within our two-week limit, and was run over a slow (sl) track, which is some ten points slower than a fast track. The winner's time in the Royal Beggar race was 1:13⅘ over the slow strip. Allowing two full seconds (10 fifths) off for the difference in track condition, the winner's time is adjusted, for comparison, to 1:11⅘. But, Royal Beggar was beaten by eleven lengths, so his adjusted fast-track time would be 1:14 which is nine points slower than his beat time as shown in the Index. We cannot qualify him on condition.

By the same process, we have to disqualify Double Disc, whose last race was adjusted from a muddy (my) track race and found to be eleven lengths slower than his best Index time.

A mere glance at Tamboro's finish (4th race) tells us the story. He was beaten by thirty lengths. A nonqualifier.

After adjustments for distance, which we'll go into in a later chapter, we were able to qualify Coylind in the fifth. And Loil Roil in the sixth. In the seventh, Big Patton was found to be ten and a half lengths slower (in his race on January 30) than his Index time. Not qualified.

In the eighth, Little Atlas checked out (in his race on January 27) to be nine lengths slower than his best time as shown in the Index. Not qualified.

Fortunate Isle had not raced since December 30, but had worked on January 29, so we checked her last race against her Index time and found her to be off nine lengths.

So here is our revised list of speed horses after making them qualify to certain standards of condition.

2	Austin Venn	$9.40	$5.20	$3.60
5	Coylind	5.40	3.60	3.00
6	Loil Roil	...	5.20	4.20

I hardly need to labor the vast differences, profitwise, in these two comparative lists.

But I do not offer this as a system. Not yet—though you and I together will develop a full-fledged system from this basic premise before we are through. No, all this is for now is an illustration, not only of the potency, and necessity, of present qualified condition, but of the kind of pitfall the uninitiated fan can stumble into if he blindly assumes that a speed-burner always has his speed.

CHAPTER TWO   *Percentages*

Speed comparison is by no means the only way to gauge the condition factor. It is a good way, but not the only way. We have already mentioned those people who can assess present, on-the-spot sharp condition simply by observing the beastie in the paddock before the race. It has something to do with the sleekness of the coat, the alertness of the eyes, and general deportment.

If I seem to be vague about this, it is because the people who claim to be able to read the signs are vague with me when I ask them to explain it to me. Perhaps it's a sixth sense you either have or do not have.

I, quite frankly, cannot tell how sharp a horse is simply by looking at him. I have to judge it the hard way. I have to analyze recent performance in actual competition and in works, and compare this with what I believe to be the established norm for the animal, that is, his performance when he *was* in good form

Admittedly, this leaves a gap. If I could close this gap, I would undoubtedly be able to pick the winner in every race. Since I cannot, I have done the next best thing. I have maneuvered the percentages in my favor.

We saw this at work in the first chapter, where we did not

attempt to uncover any new prospects in the second part of our example. But we did knock out six losing races. Avoiding potential losers, then, is every bit as important as wooing potential winners. It spells the difference between a losing day and a winning day.

There were doubtless other valid plays on this day at the Fair Grounds. We did not look for them. We were only interested in demonstrating a point: the importance of validating a potential investment on a condition basis. Since we are not gamblers, you and I, we do not intend to risk our capital on unwise investments. We are always going to demand that the percentages be in our favor.

And as long as we keep the percentages in our favor we are going to have consistent profits from our horse-track investments.

Remember, always, that condition alone is not the whole answer. Essentially, it is the validating factor. If we isolate a horse that has shown superior speed, or superior class, or superior consistency, and we can also convince ourselves that he is now at or near peak form, we then—and only then—have a sound and solid investment. We have the percentages with us.

Any time we do not spend the time and energy to make certain the percentages *are* with us, we are gambling. We are putting our reliance on luck. And Lady Luck is a very fickle dame, indeed. She may smile on you today—I do not say that she will not—but tomorrow, or the next day, or during the weeks to come, she will be so busy spreading her favors around among the many other bettors that she'll have no time for you.

No one has ever beat the races consistently by relying on luck. No one ever will. For no matter how much money you may win today, it will not be enough to sustain you through the days to come when you will not be lucky.

So let's leave luck to the gamblers. With the percentages in our favor, who needs it?

There are many ways to get percentage in your favor. For instance, I once met a man who accomplished it in his own way and was quite satisfied with his system.

He concentrated on isolating the one sure loser in a field containing no more than five starters, then played each of the other four to win. Although his percentage of winning races was fabulously high, his percentage of yield was small and his action necessarily limited. But he played large enough sums so that he had a satisfactory, worry-free livelihood. Or so he told me, and I have no reason to doubt it, for he definitely had the percentages going with him—and by the simple process of picking a loser.

Such a system has no appeal for me, personally—but every man to his fancy. I pass it along as a matter of interest, and as another example of what can be accomplished by getting the percentages to work for you. It never hurts to take a peek at how the other half lives. A system player will investigate many methods before he finds the one that seems made to order for *him* or *her*.

No matter what approach you may eventually decide upon as your very own, it should have condition as its validating factor. So let's investigate the various ways we can estimate condition from the past performance figures supplied either in the *Daily Racing Form* or the *Morning Telegraph*.

Most inexperienced fans assume that a horse which won his last race is in top form. Actually, all this shows us is that the horse *was* in winning form at that time. He cannot be assumed to be at peak now, especially if the race was run more than two weeks ago. But even if he is being sent to the post again within the two-week limiting period, we should never jump to the conclusion that he is in condition to win again today.

He may have left his winning effort on the track. In fact, so few horses come back to win a second time in a row, that many systems automatically disqualify a last-time winner.

The reason for this notorious inability to repeat a winning performance is that in winning the hide expended so much of his keen edge that he is now on the down side of his condition curve. In short, he shot his bolt to win that last one. It may be many weeks, even months, before his trainer can bring him to hand again for another winning effort.

If the trainer rests him long enough to recharge his batteries after that winning effort, then he has lost his edge through inactivity. If he brings him back too soon, the nag is too used up to give a good account of himself.

These are general remarks, to which there are exceptions. For instance, there are times when a trainer will give his horse an "easy" race prior to asking him the question. And sometimes the horse will "run in" in much slower time than he is capable of when at peak. In such case, this "easy" race has not taken his edge. On the contrary, it has acted as a tightener. He simply won an easy one while getting sharpened up to win a tougher one.

On the other side of the picture—though this is not as likely to happen as it is the other way—the trainer is able to find such an easy spot for his recent winner that he wins another, but this one in much slower time than the first. Usually, however, after a win the horse is required either to move up a notch in class, or take on some additional impost. Added weight can tend to slow him down a little more and classier competition, chances are, will set a little faster pace, so the hide's chances of repeating under these circumstances are lessened considerably.

Thus, backing a last-time winner for no better reason than

that he did win his last race, and therefore *appears* to be in top shape, can be most disconcerting.

Well, then, how about the nag that ran second or third last time, especially if not badly beaten? It's pretty obvious, even to the novice, that this piggie was pretty sharp, too.

True. Here again, it depends to a large extent on how he earned that place or show money. If it was a driving finish, in which the jock was actually trying to get to the leader before they went under the wire, the in-the-money horse may have been as nearly used up as the winner. He, too, may now have to be brought to hand again, without even the virtue of having collected the winner's share of a purse.

One of the most distressing features of this kind of "obvious" form, aside from its being misleading, is that too many inexperienced people can see it. Consequently, the horse may be underlaid. And playing underlaid horses, fellers and gals, is not the way to beat the races.

An underlaid horse, in case you're new and puzzled, is one that's been bet down below its actual chances of winning. An overlay, conversely, is a horse that has been overlooked in the betting and is going to post at odds higher than his real chances to win would indicate.

Naturally, it's the overlays that fatten the bankroll. An overlay is a bargain. An underlay is a pain in the wallet.

I do not mean to convey the impression that all short-odds horses are underlaid. It's quite possible, on occasion, that a particular horse in a particular race is a good bet at any odds— if you are willing to take what amounts to a little interest on your investment. There is, however, no absolute mortal cinch in any horse race. Even Man o' War lost one. Personally, I find it not nearly so painful to lose on an overlay as on an underlay.

But to get back to the obvious, visible condition of a horse that won his last, or ran second or third close up. The only satisfactory way to determine if he was used up in this effort is by a speed comparison such as we used in our example in the first chapter. There is another thing to consider, too, when backing a horse that has showed obvious condition in that recent last race. We are almost certain to be backing an underlay if we qualify him. For not only will the half-smart handicappers *see* that win or near-miss, and get on what they are immediately convinced is the gravy train, but many of the so-called experts—the public handicappers—will pick this animal that has shown recent good form. Thus, even those fans who admit they know nothing about picking winners and therefore turn to the experts—who supposedly know what they're doing —add the weight of their wagers to the process of beating the price down.

This is not always the case, especially if the lasttime winner appears to be taking a prohibitive jump in class, but, as you've heard, exceptions only go to prove the rule. Usually, you can expect to take the worst of the price.

For instance, I'm looking at a hide named Gal o' War. In her last race, only five days ago, she ran second, beaten by only one and a quarter lengths. This was in a six-furlong sprint at Fair Grounds. She closed strongly in that race, coming from fifth place at the head of the stretch to close four lengths in the run to the wire. She is being asked to go the route today—one and one-sixteenth miles. Even though she shows nothing but six-furlong races in her past performances, and even though she is being asked to lug four more pounds than last time, and even though she had not won a race in eleven starts, she was bet down from 5 to 1 in that last race to 3 to 1 today. Sure—on the strength of that so obvious sharp finish in her last race.

Actually, she was a good bet at 3 to 1, but you can bet the

bottom of your pocket John Q. Public did not really know he was beating the price down on a solid mare. What he saw was that she ran second, last time out. Actually, it was a much slower race than she was capable of. She was definitely not used up making such an effort. She had plenty left to make it a winning effort this time. But the point I'm trying to make is that if she had not given away her sharp condition by running second where everybody could see, her odds would undoubtedly have been 7 or 8 to 1, and she would have won just as convincingly at this overlaid price.

If her trainer had given her this tightening race in a tougher contest, she would have finished way back yonder, given away no obvious hint as to her sharpness (while running just as strong a race from a speed standpoint), and enjoyed a win this time, at long-shot odds.

These are the things you and I are going to study about condition—obvious and otherwise. For part of our job of beating the races is beating the price. It's part and parcel of getting the percentages to working for you—getting a sufficiently high percentage of winners at sufficiently high mutuels to guarantee a consistent profit.

Once the fan understands the why and wherefore of these basic essentials, he is well on his way toward amassing his first million, if that's what he's after—and who isn't? Without an understanding, from a thorough background, of what makes racing tick, he will not be able to make even a good system work.

So don't be a chap I met who had read some of my magazine articles along with some by other writers. He told me quite frankly that he never read any of the prose explaining the *reasons* for doing thus or so; he turned immediately to the summary of rules governing the system play, and took it from there.

He had been searching for *the* system for twenty years, and was still in a hurry to find the million-dollar method. He still did not comprehend that it is vital to know *why* certain things happen, and *why* certain steps must be taken to counteract or avoid these booby traps He was so busy, and so anxious, to run a deuce into a million that he defeated himself by refusing to take the time and trouble to learn and understand background.

The record books are full of failures, in all manner of businesses, that are directly traceable to a lack of understanding and know-how of the many angles and gimmicks that make the difference between profit and loss for any specific business.

A cold, basic set of rules for running a grocery store would not, and could not, make a successful grocer of a novice without the feel and background of the trade. Nor could this set of rules be arbitrarily used to operate a filling station successfully.

Then why should a man with an otherwise lucid mind think he should be able to beat the races with no better equipment than a cold set of system rules? Rules that he does not even understand the reasons for, and hence doesn't know how to apply them properly.

To give the devil his due, this man once actually ran a small amount of capital into nearly eleven thousand dollars in about three weeks' time. He bought a Cadillac, rented a nice apartment, and threw the doors wide open to his so-called friends. In short, he really tied one on. Why not? He had it made, didn't he? He could go back any time and make some new money when he ran out of the old.

That's what he tried to do. But he was never able to make

the thing work again—for the simple reason that he didn't understand why it had worked in the first instance. He did not know his background.

This point is so important that we feel impelled to cite another example, this time in an entirely different field. This man decided he wanted to be a writer. He had a good education. He could write English in a literate manner, he had done a normal amount of reading, and he felt that he had a story to tell.

He wrote his story and sold it to the now defunct *Collier's*. He had arrived on his first and only effort. Since he was obviously a natural-born writer, why should he waste his time studying the findings of the masters who had gone before him? He was a genius in his own right. All he had to do was write more stories as the spirit moved him.

He did, too. Hundreds of them. And he never sold one again, because he did not know his craft. He did not know, or care to learn, the angles and gimmicks, and the craftsmanship, that make all the difference between saleable and unsaleable fiction. His one-shot yarn just happened to have some of the right ingredients. From then on, Lady Luck was busy elsewhere.

But doesn't everyone have to start without knowledge and experience? Without experience, yes. There is only one way you can get racing experience and "feel," and that's at the racing wars—under fire. But you can prepare yourself by learning background and know-how from those who have been through the wars. You will not learn it by skipping everything but the rules summary.

To preclude this, we are not going to present any rules summaries in this tome. To get the meat of a system so that you can use it, you will have to study the whole chapter in which it is presented, and thus be exposed, at least, to the reasons and background justifying the existence of the system.

And each one of the systems presented, whether they happen to appeal to you personally or not, will be based on some factor or premise that you will need in your background if you are to understand how to make your personal million at the races.

Even if you are making a study of racing solely as a hobby, an entertaining avocation for your free time away from the job, you will want the *whole* story. But I do not have to belabor the hobbyist, for he is motivated by a keen and avid thirst for knowledge about his hobby rather than for monetary gain from it, as in the case of the man who only wants to read the rules summaries.

I am often amazed, for instance, at the intricate and detailed knowledge possessed by the radio ham. Though he may never expect to turn this knowledge and ability into financial gain, and though his status may be strictly amateur, he has nevertheless delved so deeply into his subject that he can qualify as a professional expert in radio any time he chooses.

It is paradoxical, perhaps, but we often bring more interest, and thirst, to a hobby than we do to the vocation that must in most cases support the avocation.

So, since condition is so vitally important, let's delve into some of the ways to uncover it, even though hidden to the unpracticed eye.

CHAPTER THREE *Keeping Control*

Unknown to the average fan, a horse will often start to display his nearness to peak condition by running on the pace, or close to the pace, in the early stages of a race, even though he chucks it and fades back out of contention in the later stages.

Watching for this has a double-barrel value. Not only can we often detect return to peak condition before the uninformed two-buck bettor can, and thus catch him as an overlay, but we are automatically going along with a forward-running horse, one that's in a good position to win if he can deliver when the real racing starts—in the stretch. Though we are quick to admit that the come-from-behinder, that phantom racer who suddenly appears out of nowhere to run over tired horses in the drive to the wire, is an excitement producer of the most titillating variety—the fact remains that he does not win many races. Too often, he encounters a traffic pattern too close to home that he cannot overcome. Or, to avoid this, his jockey has to take him to the extreme outside, losing valuable lengths that more often than not cost him the race.

For the newer fans, when we say a horse is "on the pace," we mean he is leading his field at that particular stage of the race. If we say he is "forcing the pace," we mean he is running

a close second and making the leader extend himself to maintain his lead. If he is "close to the pace," he may be third,
fourth, or fifth, say, but within a couple of lengths of the
leader. In such a case, he is said to be "in contention." In other
words, he is close enough at this point to contend for the lead
if he, or his jockey, so choose.

On the other hand, in a strung-out field, the third horse may
be six or seven lengths behind the leader. This far back, even
though he is running third, he can hardly be said at this point
to be in contention. When, and if, the front runner tires and
"comes back" to his field, then the third horse may come into
contention through no exertion of his own.

This brings up an interesting point in connection with that
sensational come-from-behinder. He is an optical illusion. To
all intents and purposes, he appears to have suddenly called on
a hidden reserve of speed. Many race callers will mistakenly
describe this as a belated rush. Actually, it will prove to be his
slowest quarter of the entire race. The others are simply tiring
faster than he is. If there is such a thing as a mathematical
certainty in racing, it is that the final quarter of any race will
be the slowest for each and every horse competing. The come-
from-behinder's final quarter will just not be quite as slow as
those of the horses that "come back" to him.

I first got the idea of checking the running positions in the
early stages of a race from a chance meeting with an efferves-
cent fan at the old Caliente track outside of Tia Juana, Mexico,
one Sunday afternoon.

This lad was definitely feeling no pain, and didn't care who
knew it. No, he wasn't going up against tequila and lemon, the
traditional bottled anesthesia below the border. It was the
monotonous regularity with which he was visiting the cashier's
window that had caused his spirits to soar.

Obviously, he had made a momentous discovery anent the pleasurable pastime of picking winners. Just as naturally and effortlessly as though he had been doing it all his life, he came up with the right answer in race after race—and there are twelve races carded of a Sunday afternoon at Caliente.

My curiosity won over a natural reticence, and he proved quite willing to satisfy it.

In making his amazingly successful run of selections, all this lad was doing was checking the first "call" in the past performances of each beastie in its last race. He would take for the right one the hide that had got away the most alertly in that effort. He reasoned that to get away alertly—more alertly than the others, that is—the beastie must have been on edge, the sharpest of this particular band at that time.

That, fellers and gals, was his system, in toto.

My first reaction was one of letdown. The man was balmy, a nut being blessed by a hot run that could not occur again in ten years. I've seen them at the crap table, too, exhorting Little Joe the hard way and making it seem easy and inevitable.

But it's not easy to ignore a winner, especially at the prices this man was getting which as often as not ran to boxcar proportions. So I promised myself I would research the idea a bit when time became available. There just might be something in it.

Eventually I did. I will not say I was disappointed, for I fully expected that such an incomplete thought must necessarily fall flat on its face when put to the acid test of a protracted workout. But even after abandoning it, the feeling persisted that there *was* a trace of sanity in the idea, and that if properly developed it might be used profitably.

After all, any system, even a poor one, is better than no system at all; at worst, it will minimize losses, over which the fan has no control when he chunks it into the yawning maw of the Mutuel Monster haphazardly.

So there is a point to paste in your hat as an integral part of your racing background. In your speculative activities, there must always be *control*.

Personal judgment, for 95 per cent of the fans—which all too often is nothing more than guesswork, or hunches—will prove faulty in the clutches. The noise, excitement, and pressures of the racetrack hardly make up an atmosphere conducive to sensible decisions—or to a trustworthy hunch, if there is any such thing. Most frequently, a hunch is nothing more or less than the result of indigestion brought on by too many stale hotdogs, or too much cold beer.

The system, then—or, for the handicapper, the systematized procedure of his analysis—replaces personal judgment, guesswork, or hunch by a definite control. It is true that the very regidity of a given system's controls may at some time or other compel the player to accept a selection that borders on idiocy. Still, if it is a valid system—and there are many good ones— the controls are there to bring the percentages into line, and they will do so if the system is adhered to. This, alas, is where most fans fall down. The average horseplayer is an incurable tamperer, particularly when he possesses a *little* knowledge.

Let's take a coldly jaundiced look at the lad's Caliente System. Caliente, incidentally, translated from the Spanish, means *warm*. And this lad was warm to this extent: He thought he had hit on a simple device to point up sharp condition. The device was so simple, unfortunately, as to be incomplete and inconclusive.

An alert start is fine. It precludes the necessity to make up lengths lost in a slow start. But it is not enough to assure us that our horse is in the kind of condition that will permit him to carry this good start to a successful conclusion. That alert start may mean nothing more significant than that the *jockey* was alert.

Even though the Caliente System was a dud, to know of it is of value to the student of racing because it points out how close a fan can come to a right answer and still miss the mark by a wide margin. While the Caliente System was based on the all-important premise of sharp condition, the method for determining this was faulty. Had the lad combined the alert start with a creditable running of the balance of the race, he could have developed a much more consistent wage earner.

Let's take a look at the same day at Fair Grounds, which we used as our exercise in the first chapter, this time using the alert-starter premise.

Using this single gimmick we could qualify only three horses. In the other six races, ties existed for the doubtful honor of having had the most alert start. One of these, Dude's Belle, placed (ran second); another, Sharp Thinker, showed (ran third); and the other one ran out of the money. Three losers.

We do not claim from this that the Caliente System should be discarded because of one bad day. Let's just see if the thing would be strengthened by demanding additional assurance that the animal chosen was indeed at, or approaching, peak condition. We will scrutinize all four of his calls instead of just the first one.

For Dude's Belle, an 8-year-old mare, she was on top by one at the first call, still leading by one and one-half lengths at the half, and leading by one length at the in-stretch call. She finished second, beaten by one and a half lengths. Now, that isn't a bad picture. If her previous races had been poorer than this, we could have justly assumed that she was about to come to hand. *But,* Dude's Belle had won her last two races, the last by a mere head (h) under a straining drive. So, instead of assuming that she was just coming to hand, we would have to assume she was over the hump and staling off.

For Sharp Thinker, although his first call was on top by half a length, his second call was second by half a length, his third, or in-stretch, call was fourth by two and his finish was fourth by five and three-quarters—a steady fade after an alert first quarter. Could *you* convince yourself, in the face of such evidence that this horse was in condition to win today?

After a good beginning, the third horse, Full of Joy, showed even less liking for the task at hand. At the quarter (first call), he was leading by half a length; at the half, he still retained his half-length lead; at the in-stretch call he had come all unraveled and was running fifth—eight and a half lengths behind the leader. He wound up eighth, beaten by a whopping seventeen lengths.

In the face of such evidence, isn't it pretty obvious that the alert-starter idea, made to stand all alone, leaves considerable to be desired? And yet, it was authored by a man who was supposedly aware of the importance of present sharp condition. One can only assume that he was trying to make it *too* simple. And by his parsimony, all he produced was a one day's wonder.

Still studying visual condition, let's look at the last race of the horse that beat Dude's Belle. (You will recall that Austin Venn was the speed horse we validated by speed comparison in our exercise in the first chapter.)

At the quarter call, Austin Venn was running third, four and a half lengths behind the leader; at the half, he was running second, two and a half lengths back; into the stretch, he was on top by one. He won going away by two and a quarter lengths. Yes, a last-time winner, but he won in slower time than his best time for this distance, so we don't have to worry about his having been used up. The reason we got $9.40 on an obviously sharp horse was because he was moving up $500 in claiming price by virtue of that last-race win. The gravy-train riders, some of them at least, were undoubtedly scared off by this.

Though the real condition clincher in this race was the speed comparison, the steady, relentless improvement from call to call showed by Austin Venn for all to see was stronger than the pattern shown by Dude's Belle, who went out on the pace but did not have enough edge left to withstand a determined drive in the stretch, where the real racing takes place.

So, here we have another valuable condition test, the general and steady improvement from first call to finish—and the horse need not necessarily have been running in contention at any of these calls. As an example, in the second race at Fair Grounds, on February 1, 1962, we find a 4-year-old colt named Pat's Folly. In his race on January 19, within the fifteen-day requirement, which in itself is a condition indicator, he was running sixth, eight lengths back at the quarter; at the half, he was sixth, seven and a half lengths back; into the stretch, he was still sixth, but only four and three-quarters lengths behind the leader. He finished fourth, beaten by only two and a half lengths.

Off this closing race—and it was even stronger than it appears from the visual pattern, for it was only two and a half lengths slower than his best time for this distance—Pat's Folly rewarded the faithful with a $32.40 win. An overlay? You bet he was.

Now, before some of you lynx-eyed fans, with a *Form* for this date open in front of you, take me to task on the Index time for Pat's Folly, let me point out that while the *Daily Racing Form*—and the *Telegraph,* too—are amazingly accurate publications, they do occasionally make mistakes. In this particular case, they neglected to give Pat's Folly credit in the Index for his best race at the distance. If you will look at the bottom line in the past performances for Pat's Folly, you will see a race at six furlongs on September 19, 1961 (at Latonia), showing the winner's time at 1:11, and Pat's Folly as having finished four and three-quarters lengths behind. That makes his time for this effort 1:12, instead of the 1:14⅕ shown in the Index.

Admittedly, Valk's best time was two fifths faster (1:11⅗), but he was obviously far off his best. Mull, the gelding that finished second to Pat's Folly, also had an excellent closing pattern, but his best time for the distance was two fifths slower than that of Pat's Folly (1:12⅖). Pat's Folly was the selection all right, fellers and gals, and a good solid one.

What I mean to point up here is this: one need not limit himself to the fastest Index time only, if the fastest is definitely not sharp now. We did limit ourselves this way in the exercise in the first chapter, but it was only to put over a point. On the other hand, if you are by temperament a spot player, then you could do worse than to qualify, or disqualify, the top Index horse only. From this point on, a reference to "index" will mean our own corrected and converted index. And there is no time like right now to bring the *Telegraph* user securely into the fold.

Though the *Morning Telegraph* does not supply an index, the information we need is there (in the Past Performances) for us to dig out—and for this valuable information even a lazy horseplayer should be willing to expend the effort. And, as will soon be seen, the *Form* user will also need to resort to this work in order to get the true picture. Soon, if he refers to the published Index at all, it will only be in order to get a general picture before making corrections and conversions. There will be occasions when he has no choice, for a published Index is not always shown for all tracks. For instance, in the Chicago issue, now open before me, both the Fair Grounds and Hialeah have the published Index. Santa Anita, also covered in this issue, does not. Nor does the Miami (Fla.) issue of the *Form* publish an Index for Sunshine Park.

So, to make your own index when none exists, or to check for accuracy, you simply run down the past performances until you find the fastest race at today's distance. These past performances may, or may not, cover a two-year period. It doesn't matter. Whatever information is available will answer our purpose.

In most cases, having to go back two years, or nearly two years, for a best time at the distance, is a little too far, anyway. Depending largely on the hide's age and the amount of campaigning he has done in the elapsed time, he may have gone back considerably in two years. But this need not worry us, for the comparison of his present speed ability (from that last, recently run race) will either qualify or disqualify him in any case.

Now there will be times when the Index (or the past performances) will not supply us with an effort at today's distance for each and every horse in the race under study. We are not compelled to select for such a race, are we? But if the ones not showing an effort at the distance should satisfy us by a visual study that they are not in good form, we can disregard them and make our ultimate selection from those that *have* gone the distance.

We expect a champion to be good at *any* distance. But we

are not dealing with champions, or near-champions, in the cheaper variety of races that are in preponderance. Many of these cheapies will be either sprinters or routers, which makes determining their capabilities, *at todays' distance*, a necessity.

There will also be times when that last, recently run race (from which we have to make our comparison) was not contested at today's distance. There are ways of adjusting this performance to our needs that we will go into in detail later. But right now, remember this: Whenever we find ourselves in doubt, we can always keep control of our over-all activity by passing up the doubtful race. And we *must* keep control at all times. Once we allow control to gravitate into the tempting but fickle hands of Lady Luck, we've had it.

There will not be a sound investment in every race. We refer to a single-horse-win play, of course. If we attempt to force, or manufacture, such a play where none exists, we are wooing insolvency. We are deliberately defeating our avowed purpose of making a million at the races.

Avoiding a doubtful play—a potential loser—is every bit as important as investing in a solid one.

It is true that there are "dutching" methods that are designed to cover play on more than one horse in a race. This will allow play in certain otherwise unplayable races, if we must have more action. But even the most all-encompassing of these will not fetch the winner in *every* race. And you are buying less for your investment-dollar when you resort to "dutching," or progression play. The percentage of yield is bound to be less when you stray away from flat play. But a million can be made from "dutching," too, so we'll have a look into it in a later chapter.

Which reminds us of the story of the dusky stablehand who had not had a winner in all day. With the nightcap at hand, he was determined to wind up the day with a winning pasteboard. There was only one sure way he knew of to do it. He went and bought a piece of every hide in the race. Back outside to watch them run, he realized he had solved one problem only to create another. He didn't know which one to root for. But he solved this too. As they pounded into the stretch-turn and drove toward the wire, he yelled, "Come on, *somethin'!*"

Before we leave this chapter, let's take a look at the general pattern of the type of beastie who begins to show us his return to form several races before he is finally ready. This is often over a span of three races, all usually run within a span of thirty days or less.

In his third race back, we'll say, he was running forwardly at the quarter call, but faded thereafter. Then in his second race back he was able to stay in contention for a half-mile before chucking it. And in his last race he ran well into the stretch (third call), but was "short" in the run to the wire.

All other factors being equal, he is now ready to deliver. It isn't always that clear-cut and obvious, but variations of this general pattern will show up from time to time to give us a big selecting edge over the average fan—and what is perhaps more gratifying, a fancy price, especially if that last, improved race did not culminate in the money. Though he appears to have quit in the run to the wire in that last race, you and I may still be able to qualify him, for we definitely have a positive improvement pattern on which to base our final judgment.

For now, it is enough to know that we can do ourselves some good on occasion by watching for such a pattern.

We now have sufficient background to start building our first million-dollar approach. As you have probably guessed, this one will be based on speed, *at today's distance* and validated by *recent condition*. It will be the first of a group of systems, or controls, that will ultimately comprise the *whole* million-dollar picture, or structure.

It will apply only to the first four races of a given card, and to sprint distances only—less than one mile.

Many of you observant fans will already have discovered certain weaknesses in the published Index. For one thing, it does not always show a best speed for every horse entered in the race under study. Secondly, these speeds are sometimes shown for other than a fast track, and are thus not equal to, and so comparable with, fast-track efforts.

In the first instance, we're going to have to be able to definitely disqualify the hides without speed shown at today's distance (either in the Index or in the past performances) before we dare attempt to qualify one that is represented as a high-speed-burner.

In the second instance, we are going to have to convert the off-track speeds shown to make them relatively equal or comparable. Roughly, there is a five-point (one full second) difference between the various conditions of off track. However, this will vary with distance; therefore, the following Speed Standards Charts (for sprint and route distances) will give us a more accurate picture.

These charts are essentially the same as those presented in *How To Pick Winning Horses,* published by The Citadel Press in 1963. They have been updated and revised in some instances, however, in the interest of greater accuracy in drawing our comparisons.

If you look at the chart on page 45, you will notice that the top line gives the distances: 2 furlongs (*2f*); 3 furlongs (*3f*); 4 furlongs (*4f*); and so on. Under these headings, and opposite the word "Fast," are the standard 12-second furlong speeds. In the next line, "Gd-Sy," for both a good track and a sloppy one it will be noted that the speeds shown begin to slow down a bit, through "Slow" and "Muddy" until we get down to the "Heavy" line, where they have slowed down a lot.

This slowdown will become even more apparent in the speed standards for the route distances, which follow on page 46.

To clarify: the standard speed for one mile, for instance, is one minute, 38 seconds, and $\frac{3}{5}$ of a second (1:38:3). The standard for one mile and seventy yards is one minute, 43 seconds, and $\frac{1}{5}$ of a second (1:43:1).

Now, to convert any distance or track condition to a readily comparable rating, we designate the speed standard at that distance and under the given track condition as zero. Thus, if the horse we are studying ran one and one-eighth miles in 1:53:2, he is awarded a zero (0) rating. If he ran it in 1:53:3, he gets a plus 1 (1) rating—$\frac{1}{5}$ of one second, slower than standard. Or, if he ran it in 1:53:1 (these all refer to fast-track

SPRINT DISTANCE STANDARDS

Track Condition	2f	3f	4f	4½f	5f	5½f	6f	6½f	7f
Fast	:24	:36	:48	:54	1:00	1:06	1:12	1:18	1:25
Gd-Sy	:24:2	:36:3	:48:4	:55	1:01	1:07	1:13:1	1:19:1	1:26:2
Slow	:24:4	:37:1	:49:3	:55:4	1:02	1:08	1:14:2	1:20:2	1:28:1
Muddy	:25:1	:37:4	:50:2	:56:4	1:03	1:09:2	1:15:3	1:21:4	1:29:4
Heavy	:25:3	:38:2	:51:1	:57:2	1:04	1:10:2	1:16:4	1:23:1	1:31:2

ROUTE DISTANCE STANDARDS

Track Condition	Mile	1-70	1 1/16	1⅛	1 3/16	1¼	1⅜	1½
Fast	1:38:3	1:43:1	1:45:3	1:53:2	1:59:3	2:05	2:18	2:31
Gd-Sy	1:40:1	1:45:2	1:47:1	1:55:1	2:01:3	2:08:1	2:21:1	2:34:1
Slow	1:41:4	1:46:4	1:48:4	1:57	2:03:2	2:10	2:23	2:36
Muddy	1:43:2	1:48:2	1:50:3	1:58:3	2:05	2:11:3	2:24:3	2:37:3
Heavy	1:45:2	1:49:3	1:51:3	2:01:3	2:08:1	2:14:1	2:27:1	2:40:1

speeds, of course), which is ⅕ (⅕ second) faster than standard, his rating would be minus 1 (−1). Thus, a minus rating will always be faster than a plus rating or a zero rating. And a zero rating will be faster than a plus rating.

Now, let's convert an off-track rating, just to be sure you all follow—and to a few of you, alas, who may not yet have read *How To Pick Winning Horses*, this method of comparable ratings will be new.

On February 1, 1962, in the first race at the Fair Grounds, the Index shows Lucky Love with a speed as follows: Dec61 FG 1:17 m. This means, of course, that in December of 1961, Lucky Love raced six furlongs in one minute, seventeen seconds, in the mud. Referring to our Sprint Standards chart, we see that standard for six furlongs in the muddy going is 1:15:3. This is 7 points (⅖) faster than Lucky Love's time. Taking the standard as our zero point, we thus can assign a plus seven rating to Lucky Love.

In this same race, Gold Robin has the fastest, fast-track time shown in the Index, which is 1:14:1. But our speed standard for six furlongs on a fast track is 1:12. Using this as our zero point, we find that Gold Robin's time is 11 points slower than standard. So his comparable rating is a plus eleven, or 4 points slower than Lucky Love's converted rating.

But, now that we have our Standards Charts to make the needed conversions—and to put *Form* and *Telegraph* users on an equal footing—we'll abandon the published Index in favor of one of our own making.

Thus, when we take a second look at Gold Robin, we pause at his race on January 8, 1962, his second race down the past-performance line. (Since in the *Form* the past performances are presented slightly differently from the way they are given in *Telegraph*, and since each supplies a chart to aid you in correctly reading them, I refer you to them if you are not already familiar with the p. p. hieroglyphics.)

Gold Robin's second race back was contested on a heavy track. The winner's time was 1:16. Gold Robin was beaten by four and three-quarter lengths (5 points). So his time was 1:17. Consulting our Sprint Standards chart, we see that the standard for six furlongs on a heavy track is 1:16:4. From this—and remembering that the standard is always considered as zero—it is immediately obvious that Gold Robin's time of 1:17 is only one point (one fifth) slower than standard. Thus, his converted rating is plus one. This is 6 points faster than Lucky Love's converted rating of plus 7.

That, fellers and gals, is the way they finished. Gold Robin was the quite convincing winner, by one and a half lengths. Lucky Love was second. We mention this at this point only to emphasize the fact that there is a certain strength in our own converted ratings, even *before* validated by recent condition. And it amply demonstrates the value of the chart conversion work we are *all* going to do from now on. The *Form* users may still inspect the published Index first to get a general idea of the speed picture, but the real test comes as the result of our conversions.

So this is the first part of our first million-dollar system: both *Form*-ers and *Telegraph*-ers will each make his own index by chart conversion. Assuming that each fan will make his conversions accurately, he will then have a more accurate index for our purposes than the published one.

In doing this, we will discover on occasion that a horse may have been soundly beaten in the race under study but still may have turned in a fast enough time to be eligible for consideration in today's race.

Once we have checked the distance of the race under study,

and made our conversions at today's distance, we will accept as contenders those three horses with the best ratings. This is the inherent speed of the race. From these three, we hope to find the one with sufficiently sharp condition to be ready to win today. So we list these three, with the fastest one at the top:

Gold Robin

Lucky Love

Gobel, Jr.

It would do well at this point to reassert the fact that in searching out the initial contenders, we are not concerned with how recently, or how long ago, the qualifying races were run. We just want to know where the inherent speed for this band lies.

Our next step is to list the three fastest ratings made in the last, most recent, race. If this was contended within the past fifteen (15) days, it is qualified forthwith. If it was more than 15 days ago but less than thirty (30) days ago, and the contestant shows a workout (bottom of past performances) within one week, we will qualify him. If his last race was more than 30 days ago, the time, or rating, will be recorded, but labeled NR (not recent). If the rating is the same as that which earned him a place in our index, it should be labeled LR, which indicates he made his best speed in his last race. The reason for doing this is that we cannot qualify a horse for play who made his best time and his best recent condition time in his last race. It would simply be unrealistic to expect him to improve on this, or even equal it, today. Occasionally it does happen. Most usually, it does not, for somewhat the same reason that the last-time ("used up") winner does not repeat.

So the NR and LR ratings will be listed in their proper order, but only so we'll know where the last-race speed lies; they cannot be qualified for play. Their chief function, then, is to prevent us from listing (among the last-race speed merchants) some slower horse that might tend to validate one of our index horses that might, now, be too far off peak to return us a winner.

The last race may have been at *any distance*—not necessarily today's distance—and on any kind of track. If his rating off this last race is among the best three, he must then be listed opposite our index column, with identifying labels where needed (NR or LR).

Now, let's look at the last race, and affix a rating therefrom for each contestant in the race. (Actually, we will do this habitually at the same time that we are hunting out the best time for each.) We find that Gold Robin and Gobel, Jr. are tied for top honors.

Gold Robin earned 10½ for his race on January 23, well within our 15-day limit. This was at six furlongs on a fast track.

Gobel, Jr. also earned 10½ per his six furlong mud race on January 19, also within our 15-day limit.

Chuck Wagon is our third qualifier off his good (gd) track race at six furlongs on January 13. This is more than 15 but less than 30 days ago. But his latest workout was on January 6. We still list him third in the column, but label him NR.

Gold Robin	1	Gold Robin	10½
Lucky Love	6½	Gobel, Jr.	10½
Gobel, Jr.	7	Chuck Wagon	(NR)

Gold Robin, with a plus 1 index time and a 10½ last-race time, obviously has a higher potential than Gobel, Jr., who has a plus 7 index rating, even though his last-race rating is tied with Gold Robin's last-race rating.

As we know, Gold Robin won the race by one and a half lengths and paid $6.80, $4.60, and $4.20 across the board. Lucky Love was second at $13.50 for place and $12.00 for show. Neither Gobel, Jr., nor Chuck Wagon threatened.

It will be noticed that we did not require the qualifying horse to have a last-race speed within 5 points of his best speed. (That was only to put over a point in Chapter 1.) What we seek now is the best combination, or relationship, between index rating and last-race rating.

In the second race on this day (February 1, 1962) and at the same track (Fair Grounds), we have another six-furlong race. This was a claimer for 4-year-olds and upward, with weight off for non-winning three races since July 15, and so on. (It is hoped that you have a *Form* or *Telegraph* for this date open before you so you can follow each one of these steps more closely.)

After making our conversions, we find that Rapid Rebel has the best index rating (—3½) off his fast-track race at Churchill Downs on May 14, 1960. Valk is next best (—2) off his fast-track race at Detroit on July 1, 1961. Round Head gets the third place of honor (—1) for his heavy-track race at Fair Grounds on January 15, 1962.

Rapid Rebel	—3½
Valk	—2
Round Head	—1

Wha' hoppen to Pat's Folly? Because of the conversions, which we did not fully employ when demonstrating this principle (we were still dabbling with the published Index, remember?), we lose him for the moment. But "be ye not disencouraged," as the Widow Duck used to say. We'll catch him on the next go-round—that's a promise. For though he is just beyond reach for this first system, it is only one small part of our whole control complex.

To get back to the business at hand, we find from our last-race ratings that Pat's Folly, with a plus 2½ rating for his mud race on January 19, is second to Mull, who rates a zero. But Mull made his zero in his last race as well as in his previous one, so he will have to be listed with an LR label. Pretty Pam is next with a plus 5½ off her last race, which was in the mud at Fair Grounds on January 19. So here are our parallel columns:

Rapid Rebel	—3½	Mull	0 (LR)
Valk	—2	Pat's Folly	2½
Round Head	—1	Pretty Pam	5½

Since we cannot pair up anything from this, we pass the race as far as this control is concerned.

To go back to the first race a moment and clear up a point that may cause some confusion, there were two first-time starters in this race. Since there were no past performances recorded for Bat's Beau and Finger Lakes, we had to take our ratings off the most recent workouts for each. For Bat's Beau, this was a plus 24 and for Finger Lakes a plus 16, neither of which could be considered a threat in this company. So we ignored them, just as though they were not there. Had one of them earned a minus rating large enough to place with the top three index times, then we would have had to list him, but with a WO (workout) label. If there had been more than four of these, we would have automatically passed the race. This, in effect, will automatically disqualify most "baby" races early in the year. These are the 2-year-olds, who are very new and very green.

Likewise, if there are more than four nags with no time at today's distance, we will pass the race as unplayable. Or if less than four, and one looks to be in sharp condition, we will pass the race, to be considered later under one of our other control systems. If less than four, and none appears sharp, then we proceed as though they were not there. In other words, we will attempt to make a qualification from the ones who *do* have index and last-race times.

Let's go on to the third race at Fair Grounds on this same day. This is a three-furlong "baby" race, such as we've just discussed.

Three of these have never been to the post before. Four more have had only one race, which would automatically label them LR since their last race is also their best. This leaves only two horses: Lady Bright, with two races to her credit, and Come On Bruce, with three. Obviously, there is not enough line here from which to make an intelligent selection.

The fourth race, the last one that can be considered under this speed control, or system, is also a stinkeroo, but for another reason. Most of them have not raced recently enough to qualify. However, let's work it out for practice.

It's a six-furlong claimer for 3-year-olds who have not won a race since November 22.

We make our own index by conversions to ratings. Cardona is best with a minus 3 (−3), Penshoe is next (−2), and Leerado is third with a zero (0).

Cardona's last race was also his best, so he wears an LR label. Penshoe's last race was also *his* best, so again the LR label. He also has to carry an NR label, since he is unraced since January 15 (16 days ago) and his last workout was way back yonder on December 28. The number three rating on this last race was Welt, with a plus 4.

Definitely no play.

So, we qualified one horse out of the first four races and had ourselves a winner.

Let's move on to the Hialeah card. Same day, same *Form* or *Telegraph*.

The first race was a route, at one and a half miles. We pass this for possible consideration later in one of our other control systems.

The second race is a six-furlong race for maiden fillies. Ugh! One of my personal foibles is my distrust of fillies, maiden or otherwise. But the system calls for a cursory look, at least.

There are three first-time starters in here—after scratches, of course—and one of them, Wise Eva, had a 4 workout on January 31. Since this is February 1, that speedy workout was made yesterday. She would have to be listed right on top and labelled WO. That means she steals a place from some other, slower contestant that we might otherwise be tempted to qualify. Foolish Question is next best off his January 18 race at Hialeah, which earned him a plus 3½. Bright Talk gets the third spot with a plus 4, also made on January 18 at Hialeah.

So we cannot qualify Wise Eva, because her best was a workout and her last was a workout. We cannot qualify Foolish Question because his best race was also his last race. Ditto for Bright Talk. But in looking this one over for speed, we see that Foolish Question is very definitely going to be a qualifier in one of our other control systems. So stick around, huh?

We do not mean to tantalize you by referring to qualifiers in control systems yet to be studied, but we do want you to understand that there will be other chances to turn up solid investments. For now, we will have to study them one at a time, get the background and reasoning for each, and work out some actual examples together, until we can handle them alone.

Until you become adept, you will doubtless want to work each one separately. Once you have gained facility with all of them, you will find that more and more you are looking for all of them at once.

But now we're still working with our speed-conversion control. So let's look at the third race at Hialeah.

This is a three-furlong "baby" race. Twelve of them are first-time starters. Two have one race each. This is a definite pass, without further ado.

The fourth—still at Hialeah—is a $6,500 claimer for 3-year-olds (Florida-breds preferred), with weight off for non-winning, and so on. Converting to at-the-distance standards, we find that Grandpa David and Royal Boy are tied for best index with a minus 1 (—1) each. Hooky gets the three-hole honor with a zero (0).

Grandpa David	—1
Royal Boy	—1 (actually —¾)
Hooky	0

For his last race, which was at Hialeah on January 25, 1962 (1 week), Hooky gets a plus 6, which puts him on top of the second column. Grandpa David gets a plus 7 for his race on January 25 at Hialeah. Bee Bob ties with Grandpa David with a plus 7 for his fast-track at Tropical Park on January 16, which is just within our 15-day limit.

Grandpa David	—1	Hooky	6
Royal Boy	—1	Grandpa David	7
Hooky	0	Bee Bob	7

Royal Boy, second in the index colum, is not paired in the last-race column. Bee Bob, third in the last-race column, is not paired in the index column. These two are now dropped from further consideration so far as final qualification is concerned. Grandpa David is tops in the index, or basic control, column and second in the last-race, or validating, column. Hooky is tops in the validating column and third in the basic control column. As a result, Grandpa David must be accorded the edge.

If we need further assurance, we could check the jockey angle, which we have found useful before. Grandpa David again has Hartack in the irons. Hooky has a jockey switch from Korte to R. L. Stevenson. These two boys seem to alternate on Hooky, with Korte getting considerably more run out of him than does Stevenson. Are you convinced?

This might be an interesting one to watch. The wagering public installed Grandpa David as the 3 to 2 favorite. Hooky was second choice at 2 to 1.

The bell jangles. The gates slam open. And they're off and running.

At the start, it's Hi Mister taking the lead. Trim Dee is second. And Bet Bob.

At the quarter, Hi Mister is out on the pace by two and a half lengths. Grandpa David is second by two. And Trim Dee.

At the half, it's Hi Mister by two lengths. It looks like Jockey Zakoor is going to try to steal this one. Grandpa David is second, five lengths before Trim Dee.

Around the turns and into the stretch; Hartack asks Grandpa David the question and the gelding responds by taking the lead, by a head. Hi Mister hangs on to second place, four lengths before Hooky, who has driven up from sixth place.

Driving down to the wire, Grandpa David draws out to win, going away by two and a half lengths. Hooky is next. And Hi Mister third.

Grandpa David paid $5.10, $3.00, and $2.60 across the board.

So again, at Hialeah, we were able to qualify one horse in

the first four races, and again we tabbed the winner. It begins to appear that we have more than a one-track system here, for there is considerable difference between the Fair Grounds and Hialeah.

Now let's take a look at Santa Anita, the third track serviced by this issue of the *Form*. Santa Anita is the tops in winter racing in Califormia, and creates for the selector still a different variety of problems.

In the first race offered here, on February 1, 1962, we note that the distance (stated in the conditions) is six and a half furlongs.

We do not get very far in our check before we realize we will have to disqualify this race because most of them do not have a race at the distance. And those that do raced for the first time at six and a half furlongs in their last race. We pass this for later consideration under subsequent controls.

The second race is a route for 3-year-old maidens. Since we only consider sprint distances for this speed-conversion control, we also hold this one in abeyance for a later look.

The third is a "baby" race, with insufficient line for us to make an intelligent selection.

The fourth at Santa Anita is to be contested at six furlongs. We find a lot of speed in this one in our basic index. Scan the Sky has a minus 17 (−17), for instance, but a plus 3 in his last; Papa's Move has −9½ for his best but plus 11 for his last; Turales has −8 with a plus 5 in his last. The best last-race ratings were earned by Rio Hondo Boy (−1½), but way back yonder in September at Del Mar; by Drill Site for a recent race of six and a half furlongs; by Royal Arm for a race back in October at Bay Meadows; and by Harpo for a recent six and a half furlong race at Santa Anita. Harpo, incidentally, did not have a race at six furlongs on which to give him a basic conversion rating. Yet, at a glance, we can see he is in too sharp condition to ignore. In that six and a half furlong race on January 26, he was running third at the quarter, two lengths behind the leader. At the half, while fourth, he was only two and a half lengths back. Into the stretch, he was still fourth, but only one and a half lengths off the pace. And he finished second, beaten by only three-quarters of a length. While not a perfect improvement pattern all the way, he ran a very strong race where it counts the most.

Even if we hadn't already seen that we would not be able to pair up any of the speed contenders, we would be forced to pass this race because of Harpo's obviously sharp condition and his not having had a race at the six-furlong distance. That is, we pass it so far as this first control system is concerned. We'll look at it again later.

So Santa Anita gave us no selection—and thus no winner. But what is equally important, it did not allow us to back a loser. So, in our opinion, the speed-conversion system is still working 100 per cent. And our control complex *will* pick us some nice ones on this day at Santa Anita, I promise you.

So far, so good! We would hardly ask you to believe that a one-day check—even though it encompasses three different tracks in distinctly different sections of the country, different classes of competition, and different ways of management—is long-range proof of the pudding. But it *is* encouraging, isn't it? And we intend to supply ample proof for this and the whole control complex before we're through.

Not only different localities but changing seasons have their affect on certain systems. I have encountered good summer systems that would not work at all on the winter tracks. And I have seen worthwhile winter systems that come all apart at the seams with the spring racing changeover.

There has been one book that I recall offhand, which purported to furnish workable systems for the four seasons of the year—and at least one other book in which the overly ambitious author attempted to supply a different system for each of the twelve months of the year.

Oh, well—like I said, we have to take a peek at how the other half lives once in a while. When we get too self-centered or too satisfied, so that we won't at least listen to, or read, what the other fellow has to say, we may be getting ready for a Humpty-Dumpty type of fall.

To us, it seems much more worthwhile to develop an approach, a control complex, so interwoven and complementary as to be profitable at all tracks and in all seasons.

To be sure, here are some tracks and some circuits that I prefer not to play, not because I can't turn a profit there but because I can turn a better profit elsewhere. And I don't mean to imply that there might be sharp practices at these personally unpopular tracks. Rather, it is a question of incompetence at some level of the management.

Perhaps the most difficult transition is from winter to spring racing—along about April, for instance. At this time, we have the tag ends of winter racing overlapping with the openings of the various Northern and Western tracks.

To be more specific, let's take Gulfstream Park (Florida) in April. This is a splendid operation, one of my favorites, but it faces a problem in its closing weeks in April. The stables are emptying, with feverish movement of whole stables and parts of stables to spring openings in other parts of the country. This thinning out makes it more difficult, rather than easier, to develop sound selections.

It can be a difficult time, whether you remain behind with the leftovers or migrate to "greener pastures" in the North. A one-track system that may have been working well for some time will suddenly be useless—even to pick a hot dog at a weenie roast. Nor could this same system be expected to do better in the North where some of the competition may be track-weary after a hard winter campaign, and spread thin among long-rested horses that may still be carrying some winter fat.

With a sound control complex, validated as it must be by present condition, we can still make a buck whether we stay till the last dog is hung, or migrate with the early spring herd.

Now that we've stuck our neck out, maybe we'd better take a look at some April racing to see what happens to our speed-conversion control at this time.

Let's start this spring check at Gulfstream Park, shall we?—where the Meeting and the long winter of Florida racing is in its final weeks.

We'll use the *Morning Telegraph* this time by way of being impartial. For those who prefer it, this paper is flown down from New York in plenty of time for the selector to get his work done before heading for the track. The Miami edition of the *Form* is available about suppertime of the evening before.

This particular *Telegraph* is for Monday, April 2, 1962. The first race at Gulfstream is carded at six furlongs. It is a $3,500 claimer for 4-year-olds and upward: non-winners of a race since February 28, allowed 2 pounds (since January 16, 5 pounds).

Let's go to work. By Standards Chart conversion, we ferret out our three best ratings, earned at any time and in any kind of track condition covered by the past performances.

El Misterio is tops with a minus nine (—9) earned on a fast track at Tropical Park on January 14. Lillian J. is second-best with a minus six (—6) earned on a fast strip at Hawthorne on October 6, 1961. Open Case gets the three spot nod with a zero (0) for his January 15 race at Tropical on a fast oval.

El Misterio	—9
Lillian J.	—6
Open Case	0

Qualifiers off the last race are El Misterio, right on top with a plus 1; Doshay, second with a plus 2; Open Case third with a plus 3½.

El Misterio	—9	El Misterio	1
Lillian J.	—6	Doshay	2
Open Case	0	Open Case	3½

This is clearly El Misterio's race and he rewarded the faithful with a $6.50, $4.00, and $2.80 payoff across the board. Doshay was second and Lillian J. third.

Let's go back to the past performances just in case any of you are getting ready to take me to task for qualifying a beastie that *appears* to have won his last under a hard drive. It is true that he triumphed on March 23 (ten days ago) at Gulfstream Park by only a neck. *But,* his time was a full two seconds (10 lengths) slower than his best (plus 1 and —9). Right?

Incidentally, he won this one again today in a neck (nk) finish, in plus 2 time, so he may be good for another if his trainer spots him right. This one was on a sloppy track.

The second race at Gulfstream is also a sprint, this one at seven furlongs. We find three horses that have never been the distance: Easy Story, Saquestte, and Star Piper. This is an allowance race for 3-year-old maidens. Of the three unraced at the distance, Star Piper definitely ran a sharp race in his last on March 20—well within our 15-day limit. We cannot qualify him under our speed-conversion control, and we cannot ignore him on the strength of his obviously sharp condition, so we pass this one for now, to be checked again later under another kind of control.

The third is a claimer at five furlongs for 2-year-old maidens (Florida-breds preferred).

Four of these are first-time starters. Three others have started only once. Not enough line here for us to make an intelligent selection. We pass it.

The fourth race is a route that we'll check later.

So, in the first four races at Gulfstream we had one qualified selection, which was returned the winner. You will remember that we confine ourselves to the first four races and to sprint distances under this rest part of our control complex.

Now let's migrate to Aqueduct in New York, where a cold and dreary winter is giving way to spring.

In the first race, on April 2, 1962, we see that this bunch is being asked to go one mile. Since this is a route race, we pass it by to consider later under another control method.

The second race is at six furlongs. It's a $3,500 claimer for 3-year-olds with various weights off for non-winners.

After making our index conversion, Miney Myerson gets the top spot in column 1 with a plus 1. Foggy Harbor is next with a plus 8 and Ron's Boy falls into the third slot with a plus 11.

Miney Myerson	1
Foggy Harbor	8
Ron's Boy	11

Rating all the contestants now off their last races, we find Miney Myerson and Foggy Harbor tied for top honors with a plus 12 each. Fresco's 18 gives him the third place in the second column. Since neither Fresco nor Ron's Boy are paired, they are now dropped.

Since Miney Myerson had a 7-point advantage over Foggy Harbor from a best-race standpoint, and is even with this hide in the recent, last-race rated column, there can be no doubt that Miney Myerson is our selection.

After running second all the way into the stretch behind

Ron's Boy's pace, Miney Myerson took command and won going away by one and three-quarter lengths. His mutuels were $9.00, $4.80, and $3.40 across the board.

The third race was for 2-year-old maiden fillies at five furlongs; six of them were first-time starters. Pass.

The fourth race is carded as a one and one-eighth mile route. We'll pass it for now and take another look later. One qualified selection. One winner.

And so to Laurel Park, up yonder in Maryland, which is also serviced by this edition of the *Telegraph.*

To start the action here on April 2, 1962, a six-panel event is carded for 3-year-old maidens (Maryland-bred foals).

Remittance Man, with a zero (0) for his September 6, 1961, mud race at Atlantic City, gets top spot in the first column. Hidare is second-best with a plus six and Veralan is next with a plus 9.

Hidare heads the second column with a plus six, but must be labeled LR since his last was also his best. Harold Weissman is next with a plus 8 and an NR label. Veralan is third with a plus 9 and an LR label.

No play for us here. But before we leave this race we think Harold Weissman deserves a bit of comment, inasmuch as he won this event, and by twelve open lengths; yet he was unraced since November 14, 1961, and showed no workouts whatever, recent or otherwise.

Occasionally a horse is brought to hand without the fact being tipped to the wagering fans. This is sometimes done with the aid of "Jockey Cotton," which, of course, is not a jockey at all—just a forty-foot length of rope. The trainer, or one of his hired hands, is on one end of the rope and the horse in training is on the other. The horse is thus galloped endlessly in this eighty-foot-diameter circle until the trainer decides he is ready. The railbirds do not clock Jockey Cotton. So, unless you are one of those geniuses who can spot peak condition by sight in the saddling paddock, a melon-cutting takes place while you and I are looking the other way.

Fortunately, our very critical control system kept us off this race and, as we said before, avoiding playing a loser is every bit as important percentagewise as backing a winner.

Needless to say, the so-called experts didn't see anything in Harold Weissman either, with the exception of Reigh Count, of the *Morning Telegraph's* Consensus block. Neither did the coup entirely escape detection, for dear Harold was bet down to lukewam favoritism, 3 to 1.

What probably happened was this: The stable personnel, being in on the q.t. caper, were unable to control their enthusiasm and sent more money through the mutuel maw than they should have—or than was prudent—on Harold Weissman. When the odds began to drop, the smart-money speculators saw the action on the Tote Board, and got on for the ride. Thus, a horse that should have been 12 or 14 to 1 was made the favorite at 3 to 1.

We mention this only for its nuisance value and for its passing interest to you, the fan, that there is a breed of operator who takes his play direct from the money action as it unfolds before the race on the Tote Board. It is *not* a part of our million-dollar control complex.

The second race at Laurel presents a different kind of problem for our conversion control to handle. It's at six furlongs, a $3,000 claimer for 4-year-olds and upward, with weight off for non-winning since specified dates.

Cartridge makes the top spot in the first column with a minus ten (—10) off his mud race at Monmouth Park (N. J.) on July 13, 1961. Star Velvet is second with minus one and a half (—1½) for his fast-track race at Tropical on December 6, 1961. And here's where the egg hits the fan: there are no less than four horses with a best rating of zero (0) tied for the third spot—Grand Opera, Sea Tread, Debate, and Helen's Joy. With six contenders in column 1, the basic control column, this is just too much contention. It negates the tight limiting of contention that is the real strength of this particular control system. At best, it gives us a doubtful premise on which to start. So we refer to our earlier admonition—always pass a doubtful race, since it is just as much a part of our job to avoid losers as to validate the solid ones.

In an extreme case of this kind, it can be argued that the validating column might well pick one of the top two contenders. In which case, I would find no fault with a fan if he chose to do it this way—that is, list only Cartridge and Star Velvet as contenders in column 1, and see if either can be validated, or paired, in column 2.

Let's see if this would buy us anything.

Off her last race, Miss Houston gets the top spot in column 2 with a win at five and a half furlongs on a fast track at Bowie on March 26, well within our 15-day limit. Finkie gets the second spot with a plus 2 off his last race, which was on a fast strip at Bowie on March 16. This is more than 15 days ago, but Finkie had a workout on March 31, so we okay him. However, his best race was also his last race, so we have to label him LR. Since we listed only two horses in column 1, it would seem logical to list only two in column 2. And since we have no pairing, we pass the race. So our tight control system does for us what we should have done in the first place, in view of the doubtful nature of the offering.

The third race is a maiden special weight affair for 2-year-old colts and geldings. It is to be contested at four and a half furlongs and only one, Nirboy, has ever raced before.

There's no problem here. It's a clear pass.

The fourth is at six furlongs, a $3,500 claimer for 3-year-old fillies.

Ferreting out our best race at the distance for all contestants, we find that Janis Garber has the best rating off her mud race at Fair Grounds on January 19, 1962. The Start is second-best off his mud race at Rockingham on August 22, 1961. Bill's Gert and Pomp's Favorite are tied for the third spot with a zero (0) each. We are willing to stretch a point and go along with a two-horse tie, since this does not throw our contender column quite so far out of focus. But if the more conservative among you choose to list only the top two, I would be the last to censure you.

Janis Garber	0
The Start	3
Bill's Gert	6
Pomp's Favorite	6

Pomp's Favorite heads column 2 with a plus 6. But his best was also plus 6, so we must label him LR. Cross Up is second with plus 8 and Lady Daphne is third with 8½.

Janis Garber	0	Pomp's Favorite	6 (LR) (NR)
The Start	3	Cross Up	8
Bill's Gert	6	Lady Daphne	8½
Pomp's Favorite	6		

Since we cannot qualify Pomp's Favorite because of his LR label, and since none of the others pair up, we must pass the race. We got a little ahead of ourself here. As noted above, Pomp's Favorite was also NR since his last race was on March 13, more than 15 days ago, and his last workout was on January 19, more than a week ago.

You may wonder why we keep such a tight control on this

initial control system when you may already have peeked ahead and seen that we are much more elastic in other parts of our control complex. It is because in these first four races we are dealing with the cheaper grade of contestants, who are none too reliable at best. But even among these, on occasion, there is a truly solid play, so the control must be tight to keep us from backing the potential losers. After this tight weeding-out process, we can come back later and apply our more elastic tests—*not based on speed*—which may isolate additional playable nags, even among these cheap ones, for there are times when a pretty fair sort is dropped in with a band of piggies for a melon-cutting—and we dearly love melon, especially if it's of the juicy variety.

We'll explain the foregoing in more detail as our subsequent control systems unfold. For now, let us remind you that there is *a reason* for everything that happens in racing. And rarely is it obscure (once you know what to look for), as was the case with the Harold Weissman caper.

These q.t. moves are relatively few and they are more than counterbalanced through our controls by the obvious kind that go unnoticed, and therefore at fancy prices. We refer to the Pat's Folly kind of "sleeper," or one like Weeper's Boy, who also paid over $30—or, in the last race we studied, the filly race at Laurel that was won by Cross Up for an $18 payoff. A reason for this one too? You bet there was. A reason that you and I will be able to see in advance, when it counts and when most of the rest of the cash customers are looking the other way. There is no Tote Board "leak" on this kind for nobody much seems to notice, frequently not even the stable that sends the horse out. Or if they do, they're smart enough to do their betting away from the track—preferably in some distant city, through an agent, so that the track price is not affected.

All right—so now we have checked our little speed-conversion system against the early races of six different tracks, each with its own peculiarities and problems. Our initial speed control has picked four horses—and four winners. Two of the tracks, Santa Anita and Laurel gave us no action. Neither did they give us any losers.

As has been noted, we made no effort to handpick these six tracks, but took what was covered by one edition of the *Form* and one edition of the *Telegraph*. Even though it was a grab-sample and was intended to be representative, we must warn you that four for four is too much to expect for a long-term operation, even one that maintains such a tight control. Keep in mind that *nobody wins 'em all,* so that when you pick an occasional loser in making your check, you will not be disappointed. Things *do* happen during the running of a race over which we have no foreseeable control.

Sometimes horses, being high-strung, sulk. Sometimes a traffic problem causes an upset. Sometimes a jockey will make an error in judgment, thereby losing a race he should have won. More often, especially during the early part of our checkback, while we are gaining facility in handling the various controls, the error will be one of selection.

Don't let this worry you. And don't indulge in second-guessing. Go on. Your work will improve as you persevere. If you would become a virtuoso, you must practice constantly. The things you overlook at first will become second nature to you as you progress.

When you have reached the point where you are selecting 70 per cent winners, you are ready to go to the track. Not before. It is an attainable goal. It is a worthwhile goal. And a million dollars is the prize.

CHAPTER SIX

Learn by Doing

I do not intend to do all your work for you. It would do you no good even if I were willing. A year's workout, or a thousand-race workout made by me would teach you nothing. You will have to learn by doing.

But I am going to supply you with enough workouts and enough detailed examples as we go along so that you will see what to shoot for, and how to shoot for it.

Nor will you get it all with one reading of this book—unless you're one of the alert, receptive geniuses with photographic memories.

Not long ago I had a letter from one of my lady fans on the West Coast. She had a copy of my first book, *How To Pick Winning Horses.* She was on her sixth reading and was still learning new and exciting things with each rereading. What is more important, though she had been playing the races for many years, she was now, for the first time, showing a profit.

Work and perseverence! There are no substitutes.

So let's take a look at a short workout. I don't expect you to learn anything from it. Workouts are cold, monotonous things. But you may gain a little confidence from it. If you do, it has served its purpose.

Since we started with the Fair Grounds, in New Orleans,

let's be consistent. Let's see what happened during the first week in February, 1962 (six racing days), using only the speed-conversion control, of course, as applied to sprint races appearing among the first four carded events each day.

DATE	RACE	HORSE	WIN	PLACE	SHOW
2/1	1	Gold Robin	$6.80	$4.60	$4.20
2/2		[There was no qualified play this day for this control.]			
2/3	1	Hudson Kid	. . .	. . .	. . .
	4	Eternal Bim	3.80	3.00	2.60
2/5	4	Ojo Rojo	5.00	3.00	3.00
2/6		[There was no qualified play this day for this control.]			
2/7	2	{ Jacqueline J.	. . .	. . .	. . .
		{ Lepus	34.40	15.40	10.60

Note: In the second race on February 7, Jacqueline J. and Lepus were tied with a zero (0) each in column 1; they were also tied on last-race rating with a plus ten each. A mild "dutch," playing both to win, produced a fine win.

Had Jacqueline J. won it, the win mutuel would have been $7.40, which would also have produced a profit. Had these two been bet down to short-priced choices, there would have been no reason to play the race and we would have passed. As it was, with Lepus at 15 to 1, and Jacqueline J. at 5 to 2, it was a sound speculation.

So our speed-conversion control picked qualified action in five races during this first week of February, 1962, at the Fair Grounds. Only one of these failed to return us a winner. This was Hudson Kid in the first race on February 3, which only goes to prove my contention that nobody wins 'em all.

Should some of you be thinking that this is rather skimpy action—five plays in six days of racing—let me remind you that this is but one segment of our control complex.

Also, at this point, I expect some will want to challenge me to prove my statement that there is a reason for everything that happens in racing—like what was the reason for Hudson Kid's poor race?

I quote the chart caller: "Hudson Kid showed early speed but went sore during the race." This, in effect, is a polite way of saying that the trainer sent a sore horse into the race. Since the chart caller did not say "went lame" or "broke down," but "went sore," we are forced to assume that Hudson Kid was already sore, and that the strain of extending himself in the race worsened the condition to the point where he was too "hurty" to extend himself further.

This is something that may have been known to the trainer, or he may have thought the soreness was dissipated to a point where it wouldn't retard Hudson Kid appreciably. If this was the case, one wonders why there was a shift of jockeys from Phelps to Tauzin, the latter a boy who had never ridden Hudson Kid? While the jockey-switch information was available to us for what we wanted to make of it, the bit about the soreness was not. This is why I said earlier that we have to trust the trainer for last minute condition—unless we can read it direct from the hide in the saddling paddock.

It is not something to worry about—or beef about after we have to tear up a ticket—for we do have a measure of assurance from the various State Racing Commissions. In general, the Commission rulings dictate that a horse must be ready for and sent into a given race to try to win. And the Stewards at each track are there to see that Commission regulations are carried out. These gentlemen ask some pretty pointed questions if they have reason to believe there has been an attempted infraction of rules. Should their questions not be satisfactorily answered, the matter is then referred to the Commission for further investigation and, where called for, punitive action.

What we're leading up to is this: If our own investigation indicates to us that a certain horse should be in condition to win at this time, and if he is spotted with a group of contenders he should be able to beat, we are not leaving very much to chance, or burdening the conscience of the trainer unduly.

In short, if we have done our work well, we have the percentages in our favor. We have done all we can to make sure we have an "edge." If we knew positively that we could win them *all*, speculation would become a dull, monotonous business—which, believe me, it is not.

It is assumed that the student-fan will do his research chiefly for those tracks where he eventually intends to campaign. This is only good sense. For each track or circuit has its own class of competition and its own problems. By researching these tracks, we get to know their *modus operandi*, whether we're acutely conscious of it or not. In checking out our various control systems, we are bound to find that certain of them will show unusual strength at certain tracks.

Already, though it's not yet necessarily a trend, in checking out six tracks for one day each, we have seen that two of them produced no action at all for our speed-conversion system. These were Santa Anita and Laurel. From only a one-day check, we cannot conclude that a speed delineation will be relatively ineffective at either of these tracks—or I should say relatively unprofitable—to the point where one might be inclined to soft-pedal this one control at these particular tracks. But after a concerted research of what had transpired at either track in the past, we would know which of our complexes, at this particular operation, could be expected to carry the million-dollar load, and which to expect would make cakes and coffee.

For the sake of argument and example, let's say that Santa Anita should check out as a track where speed delineation is not nearly as useful as control by consistency, validated by present condition, of course. Or that one of our class controls will carry the major part of the load. The situation might be reversed at Hollywood Park or Bay Meadows—all within the California circuit.

This information is useful if that is where we plan to campaign. Years ago, when I used to hold forth on the California circuit, I found speed a very useful thing at the Santa Anita meeting. I suspect that this may not be so prevalent today, but I'm not sure for it's been some years since I was out on the West Coast. I am now more familiar with the Florida winter tracks and the New Jersey and New York summer tracks.

The point I wish to make here is that it is good sense not to walk into a "new" plant cold, without having first run off a check-back to learn where the strength is in this particular operation. I do not mean by this that the control complex will not make money at any track; I mean that it will make *you* more money if you are already somewhat familiar with the trend. It is also a matter of confidence. And confidence, fellers and gals, is something you should have with you when you go up against *any* operation.

Next, let's look at our workout for the first week in February, 1962, at Hialeah:

DATE	RACE	HORSE	WIN	PLACE	SHOW
2/1	4	Grandpa David	$5.10	$3.00	$2.60
2/2	{ 2	Island Ford	8.10	4.70	3.70
	{ 4	Gutter Ball	...	...	...
2/3	[No qualified play for our speed conversion control.]				
2/5	[" " " " " " " "]				
2/6	[" " " " " " " "]				
2/7	3	Nirisbi	...	...	2.80

Two out of four. Not very exciting, but still profitable, and only a small part of our control complex. This is why it's really futile to present more than just token workouts at this time We can show only one small corner of the picture at this point

So let's leave our speed-conversion control for the present and take a look at the second system in our control complex.

In case any of you are wondering why we present this in this way, instead of just offering a number of different and distinct systems for the student-fan to pick and choose from, it is because we have learned down through the years, the hard way, that no one system and no one factor should be expected to carry the whole load.

I have suggested in previous books and magazine articles that a fan should have a bare minimum of three systems in use at all times. To the best of my knowledge, this well-intended suggestion has not been adopted by many fans. The trouble is, they get high on some one system, and forget everything else.

I am hopeful that through my presenting this as a *control complex,* more of my friends will find the million-dollar road. What the complex amounts to, actually, is an attempt on my part to systematize, or "mechanicalize," my own processes of analysis.

Let's get on with it, shall we?

Class is quite a problem to most fans, and it is true that it covers a wide range on the quality scale, which can become pretty confusing. Class, like speed, must be considered as a relative thing. Sometimes we have to get at it on a superiority by association basis.

Speed itself is a measure of class, for whoever heard of a slow class horse? When we speak of top quality in horseflesh—that is, the champion, or near-champion—we are speaking of a very fast animal. Its speed is inherent and understood, so when we're dealing with the higher grades of runners we take speed for granted. On the other hand, with some of the groups of very cheap, or untried, horses, we must resort to a speed delineation in order to arrive at relative class, which is what we did in applying speed to the sprint-distance cheap races, among the first four of a day's card.

While we were working with the speed factor on these races, we were accomplishing something else. In those races where we could not qualify, or validate, a hide on both speed and condition in the way we were using them, we may have noticed some other things.

For instance, did you notice that in some of those cheap claimers—and maiden races, too—there was often apparent a

sprinkling of classier events in the past performance class line?
Be thinking about it.

There are, of course, grades within grades, which helps to
confuse the newer fan. Generally speaking, though, there are
claimers, maiden races, allowance races, the handicap races of
the overnight variety, and the big-name handicaps or stakes.
All of these latter are identified in the *Form's* past performances as HcpS. In the *Telegraph*, they are given their proper
name, followed by a capital *H*. Thus, Broward *H*. Or Jasmine
H. Or Flamingo *H*. Where you see such a proper name not
followed by the capital *H*, the reference is to lesser handicaps
(not stakes) and name allowance races that may have been
stakes. These would be designated as HcpO in the *Form*.
Also in the *Form*, you will note such designations as SS. These
are scale-weight stakes, and they are used to separate the men
from the boys in the juvenile circles. The WfaS, or weight-for-
age stake, is the derby.

There are also many grades within grades among the many
allowance races carded. Some of them are quite cheap, while
others may attract competitors from the stakes ranks. Generally speaking, though, an allowance race is regarded as a
better class event than a claimer and of less lustre than the
stakes events, which, as you will see, is close enough for our
purpose.

Even among the lowly maidens there are grades within
grades. There is the plain maiden race, the maiden special
weight, the allowance maiden, and there is also the maiden
claimer. This one is considered at the bottom of the ladder in
the maiden category, with the AlwM at the top.

So what we probably noticed, I hope, as we worked with
speed conversion, was that some of these higher grade classifi-
cations cropped up on occasion in the class lines of some of the
hides in these early and cheap events.

It is this area that we are now going to explore.

Any race of those first four that may have yielded us a play on speed conversion will not come in for scrutiny on this our class-plus-condition exploration. Since speed gave us Gold Robin in the first at Fair Grounds for February 1, 1962, we shall start our hunt with the second race, where, if you recall, we could not quite qualify Pat's Folly on speed.

It will also have been noticed that we called attention to the type of race when exploring for speed, even though, at that point, we were primarily interested in whether it was a sprint distance. But this is a good habit to form: *always read the conditions* before starting your search of the past performances. They may not mean too much to you at first, but the cryptic language will come to have a special meaning for you after a time. And knowing what the conditions are for this race makes you more receptive to the kind of analysis this one needs. Forming this simple working habit gives you an "edge" over the fellow who never reads conditions.

Now, we are no longer looking solely for sprint races. What we want from the conditions, which control the class of entry, is the type of race we are about to study.

In the second race, then, the conditions tell us this is a claiming race for 4-year-olds and upward. Just knowing this much about this race tells us where we must look for possible contenders.

No, we are definitely not going to get involved in the idiocy of juggling claiming price tags. But since this *is* a claiming race, and a cheap one ($2,000), we are going to be interested in any contestant who shows, somewhere in his past performance line, that he has been exposed to a better type of race. We do not care how well he did in this better type race—only that he was entered in it.

Lost Chord, Pretty Pam, and Valk show nothing but claimers in their respective past performances. Du-Ni was out in an allowance (Alw) race at Jefferson Downs on November 15, 1961.

Pat's Folly had an outing in allowance company at Latonia on October 5, 1961. Round Head shows nothing but claimers in his class line. All Red had an allowance race at Thistledown on September 29, 1961. Three Grand, nothing but claimers. Rapid Rebel had two allowance races at Thistledown. Connie Cat and Mull shows nothing but claimers.

Our contender group, then, are those horses that have raced, at some time in the past, in a better grade of competition than they're meeting today.

These are Du-Ni, Pat's Folly, All Red, and Rapid Rebel. Of these, we toss Rapid Rebel out at once because she has not raced for more than two years. Our 15-day rule remains intact. This is always the first step in condition delineation, that, to qualify, the horse must have raced within fifteen days of today's date.

Our job now is to determine which of the remaining three contenders is in condition to win this race. For this purpose, we can use any of the condition indicators we have already studied, plus one more that is a very useful gimmick indeed.

This one has to do with the finish calls in the last two races. The last one must, of course, have been run within our 15-day limit. The previous one, the next to last, is the most meaningful if it was contested within the last thirty days, but we do not make this a must. For no matter when it was run, a comparison of it with the last race that was run within fifteen days will tell us a good deal about the hide's recent condition.

Regardless of finish position—whether he wound up second, fifth, or umpteenth—it is the number of lengths involved that interests us. The number of beaten lengths in the last race must be *less* by *more than a half-length* than the beaten lengths in that previous race. Now then, if he won both the last two, he must have won the last by more than he won the other—again, in excess of half a length.

To put it another way, if the horse under study was beaten by more lengths in his last race than in his previous one, he is not sharp enough for our purpose. Or, if he won the last by a small margin and the previous by, say, three or four lengths, we are not interested in him today.

Just in case some of the newer hands may not quite understand about lengths, or rather where and how to read them, they are the small upper-case figures given in conjunction with the larger running-position figures for each call. In the past performances, the upper-case figures given in both *Form* and *Telegraph* indicate lengths behind the winner at the finish call, or lengths off the pace at that point for the other calls. This holds for reading the past performances only. Reading a *chart* of a given race, the small upper-case figures still refer to lengths, but lengths ahead of the next horse instead of lengths behind the winner, or leader.

Since we will be concerned only with past performances, not charts, there should be no difficulty. I mention it merely because this does seem to be a point of confusion for some fans.

This new gimmick, the comparison of the last race finish with the previous race finish—which we will refer to as "l/p" from now on—is the prime visual factor. Actually, it carries more weight than the excellent first-call-to-finish improvement pattern in this kind of determination, but this should not prevent us from observing the other indicators also.

Let's work some examples. We'll start with our first contender in the second race at the Fair Grounds. This was Du-Ni.

Du-Ni raced last on January 25, 1962, at Fair Grounds, which is well within our 15-day limit—this being February 1, 1962. At the first running call, he was tenth, seven and three-quarter lengths behind the leader at that point; at the second call, he was eleventh, seven lengths back; at the in-scretch call, he was tenth, nine and three-quarter lengths off the pace. He finished sixth, six and a half lengths behind the winner. Inasmuch as he closed well from the in-stretch call to the finish, we can assume that he was shuffled in the crowding coming around the bend, where he lost almost three lengths. To be able to come on again and make up—more than make up—the ground lost coming around the turn, indicates that this horse has condition in his favor. Otherwise, he could not have closed in that determined manner. But when we apply the acid test— the 1/p—we eliminate Du-Ni from further consideration.

In that last race, he was beaten by six and a half lengths. In the previous one, he was beaten by only five lengths. Therefore, since he did not improve his finish in the last race over the previous one, we decide he still lacks that winning edge.

Pat's Folly is next. Some of you will doubtless recall that we used Pat's Folly as an example to demonstrate the first-call-to-finish pattern of near-peak form. In case you don't, Pat's Folly was running sixth, eight lengths off the pace at the first call (that's the first running call, you *Telegraph*-ers, not the "at start" call); at the pre-stretch, or second call, he was sixth, seven and a half lengths back; around the bend and into the stretch he was sixth, four and three-quarter lengths behind the leader. He finished fourth, beaten by only two and a half lengths. This, of course, is a closing pattern all the way. Not sensational, but there was a steady, relentless quality about it. Certainly it speaks loudly for approaching peak form for Pat's Folly. From a speed standpoint, we will doubtless remember that this colt was only two and a half lengths off his best in this one. And from a quick glance down his finish line, we see that there has been no recent win from which he might still be recovering or staling, as the case may be.

Now we apply the acid test, the good and reliable 1/p. Pat's Folly's last race, incidentally, was on January 19, which is within our 15-day limit. His previous race was also in January, and within thirty days, on the 3rd. In this one, he was beaten by fourteen lengths. In his last, he was beaten by only two and a half. So he is qualified on 1/p also.

All Red, our next contender, had a closing pattern from the pre-stretch (second) call to finish, making up some eleven and a half lengths to be beaten six and a half lengths. There is evidence of condition here, though his bad beginning tends to bury the fact. Also, All Red was five and a half lengths off his best at this time, and his best (plus 9) leaves a good deal to be desired, especially in a sprint race.

Then, in applying our 1/p, we find that while All Red did in fact improve his finish, it was by only a half-length. And we require the improvement to be *more* than a half-length.

Had we not already tossed out Rapid Rebel on the time limit, she would now have fallen by the wayside on the 1/p gimmick.

From the above, it should be quite evident that Pat's Folly gets the nod on class-condition control.

His mutuels, in case you have forgotten, were $32.40, $9.00, and $6.40 across the board.

To win this one, Pat's Folly showed the same kind of closing pattern as in the race in which he told us he was about ready to win.

The third race was the 2-year-old maiden claimer that we were forced to pass in our speed-conversion control. We cannot work it on class-condition control, either—not this phase of it, at least, and probably not at all—for too many of them do not yet have as many as two races. We need a minimum of two for our 1/p test.

In the fourth race, another six-furlong claimer, we have four possible contenders, until we apply the 15-day limit. None of them qualifies on this first step so there is no need to do any of the other work. But for the record, the almost-contenders were: Pine Fire, with 6 Alw and 1 AlwS in her class line; Welt with 3 Alw; Cordona with 2 Alw; and Lucy's Reward with 1 Alw and 1 AlwM. It should be stressed here that we are not using the recent workout, as we did with speed conversion, to bring a horse into the contender group, if he had raced within the supplemental 15-30-day limit and had worked within one week. We feel that we are being elastic enough in our basic grouping without adding any more leeway.

The fifth race is a filly and mare race for 4-year-olds and upward. It is another cheap claimer ($2,000), to be contested at one and one-sixteenth miles.

None of these has ever raced in anything but claiming affairs, so we have no contenders for this kind of control.

By that, I mean there are no class contenders. But it is interesting to note that Gal o' War, Little Shawnsie, and Harlyn Miss showed good condition indicators, with Gal o' War earning brackets at the wire. This would have been a spot for action for the "dutching" player, if one *had* to play such a race.

The sixth race is a $5,000 claimer for 3-year-olds, to be contested at six furlongs. Note that we are now beginning to see a better quality of horses, even within the claiming grade. Some tracks will run their feature race as the sixth stanza, or a co-feature event, though most usually the seventh is carded as the day's main tussle.

Though this is still in the claiming category, we note a much more generous sprinkling of allowance races in the various past performances for the majority of the contestants. Only Brown Brother, Hawaiian Music, and Valdina's Last have not raced in some grading of the allowance category.

Of the remainder, Sun Ponder has much the best class line, with six Alw, 1 HcpO, and 1 AlwS. He shows a closing pattern from the second call to finish and a nice fat improvement in his 1/p, but he has not been raced since January 4.

The only other possible contender having a qualifying 1/p is In the Barrel, and he could not meet the 15-day limit requirement either.

Sun Ponder won the race and In the Barrel was third. We could have stretched a point and qualified Sun Ponder, in view of his superior class line and an excellent workout on January 29. But, as we told you earlier in the text, it is as much our job to disqualify as to qualify. This is a habit worth cultivating for it can keep us from backing many a loser. And a horse like Sun Ponder, at 3 to 2 odds, would not stand off many losers.

The seventh at Fair Grounds, as it turned out, was not the day's feature race. Instead, it was a $4,000 claimer for 4-year-olds and upward, going six panels.

Bonnie Pat had one allowance event, at Randall Park (Ohio) on July 13, 1961, but was unraced since November 8, 1961. Not a qualifier.

High Bush had 7 Alw and 1 HcpO in his class line. He had raced on January 22, well within our 15-day limit. In this last race, he had been running eight, six and three-quarter lengths off the pace at the first call; at the second, or pre-stretch, call he was seventh, five and three-quarter lengths back; around the bend and into the stretch he was running sixth, but was six and a quarter lengths off the pace. He finished still sixth, but beaten by seven and a quarter lengths. There is nothing in that to indicate to us that this horse is ready.

In any case, his 1/p was negative, so his superior class line means nothing here. A horse only has his class when he is in condition, just as he only has his speed when he is in condition.

These were the only two contenders in the seventh race, so we pass.

And at last, we have arrived at the Fair Grounds' feature race. It is carded as the Dr. Peter Graffagnino Purse and is an allowance romp for 4-year-olds and upward. They are to run six furlongs.

Since we have said our search for contenders must always be in a higher classification than called out in today's conditions, which in this case is an allowance, we will have to look for horses that have run in stakes events.

Only two qualify as contenders: Royal Music and Orleans Doge.

Royal Music has one HcpS in his class line, but was automatically disqualified because his last race was way back on December 16, 1961.

Orleans Doge raced on January 27 at this track, well within our time limit. In this race, he was running third, three and a half lengths off the pace, at the first call; third, three lengths back, at the pre-stretch call; second by a head (h) as they straightened out into the stretch; and won going away by four and a half lengths. A perfect improvement pattern.

Orleans Doge won this one so easily that we could be forgiven for taking it for granted that he was not used up by the effort. But in case we want to gild the lily, it can be said that the rating he earned on the muddy strip in that last race, while a fabulous minus 17 (-17), was still two lengths slower than his best race, which was a minus 19 (-19). And as we said before, we expect a stakes racer, especially one who has campaigned on the Big Apple (his past performance show HcpS at Aqueduct, Atlantic City, and Saratoga) to be good at any distance.

This might be a good place to recall too, that we said speed and class are necessarily complementary. Where among the cheap campaigners would you find a —17 or a —19 standard rating?

So we're not through gilding the lily yet. In his previous race, on January 20—still within the fifteen days, and therefore qualified for the 30-day maximum for the second race back—Orleans Doge ran another strong closing race from first call to finish, promising victory in the January 27 event. In the previous race, he finished second, beaten by two and a quarter lengths (this after more than two months layoff). So his 1/p improvement was six and three-quarter lengths.

Orleans Doge had all the appearance of a copper-riveted, double-locked, mortal cinch. But there was something wrong with the picture: everybody could see it.

Orleans Doge was bet down to forty cents on the dollar. That's right. He paid $2.80 for another easy win. Here's what the chart caller had to say about the race: "Orleans Doge saved ground until near the stretch, moved to the outside at the turn and, taking command from Go Good when ready, won with speed in reserve."

Though it's anticlimatic after such a race, let's take a look at the nightcap which more often than not is a real stinkeroo. This is the one in which the diehards try to get well, instead of licking their wounds and waiting for another day.

The ninth race was at one and one-sixteenth miles, a $2,500 claimer for 4-year-olds and upward.

Only two hides in this affair showed anything but claiming efforts. Moon's Wave showed two HcpO at Jefferson Downs in October of 1961. Quibay showed three HcpO at the same track in October and November of 1961.

Moon's Wave showed a closing race in his last on January 20, well within our 15-day limit, but he backed up in the stretch to be beaten by six lengths, though saving second place. This would not have looked too bad had he not won his previous race in a hard neck-and-neck duel. This was on January 5, and indications are that Moon's Wave left his race on the track at that time. In any case, the 1/p is negative.

So we have a look at Quibay. He raced on January 23 at the Fair Grounds, well within the 15-day limit. This race was dull. It was neither very bad nor very good; he was beaten by almost eight lengths, slowing down two in the drive to the wire. About the only thing that can be said for the race is that Quibay certainly wasn't used up making the effort. In fact, it appeared as though he'd made very little effort at all. But we could hardly pass the race out of hand. After all, that's what we have our controls for, to make our decisions for us.

So, we check Quibay's 1/p. It's positive. He was beaten by ten lengths in his previous race, as against seven and three-quarter lengths in his last—a two and a quarter length 1/p improvement.

This is of special interest, because 1/p will so often uncover the hidden answer when nothing else will.

So Quibay qualifies, and we hope this example will help to instill confidence in you for 1/p.

Quibay won an easy race at this distance by five lengths, on December 22 at Fair Grounds. Then he ran third in a return engagement on January 3, then seventh by ten on January 2. If it had not been for 1/p tipping us off, we would have been justified in assuming that the hide staled off after his December 22 win.

As it was, we caught a nightcap win at $6.80, $4.20, and $3.20 across the board. There were two others in this waltz with 1/p improvement, but they weren't contenders.

Now, with the additional action, let's see how our February 1 work sheet is shaping up at the Fair Grounds.

RACE	HORSE	WIN	PLACE	SHOW
1	Gold Robin	$6.80	$4.60	$4.20
2	Pat's Folly	32.40	9.00	6.40
8	Orleans Doge	2.80	2.20	2.20
9	Quibay	6.80	4.20	3.20

Hmmmmm! Well, let's get on with it.

CHAPTER EIGHT

Comparison Control

To remain consistent and to bring our study along on a constantly comparable basis, we now move to Hialeah to see what happened there on February 1, 1962, when we applied our class-condition control.

The first race, which we passed up on our speed-conversion control because it was not a sprint, was carded at one and a half miles on the turf course. It's a claiming race for 4-year-olds and upward who have not won at one and an eighth miles or over since November 22. A real daisy!

Doshay has three HcpO in his class line and two HcpS, all at Sunshine Park during the winter meeting of 1961. Sunshine Park, Florida's only West Coast horsetrack, though always an interesting and formful meeting, is hardly in the same league with Hialeah, or any of the other Big Apple tracks. Therefore, Doshay's Hcp efforts must be held suspect, but we need not worry about it; our controls can be depended upon to handle the situation.

So we call Doshay a contender. He raced at Hialeah on January 25, which is within our 15-day limit. At the first call in this race, he was fourth, three lengths off the pace; at the pre-stretch call, he was tenth, thirteen lengths back; at the in-stretch call, he was eleventh, eighteen lengths out of it. He finished eleventh, beaten by twenty-nine lengths. A very dismal performance. But just out of pure contrariness we'll look at his 1/p. In his previous race—at Monmouth, a top-flight New Jersey oval—he finished seventh, by nineteen lengths. On such figures, we couldn't qualify him if he had won the Grand Prix.

In case there should be a question, let's take a look at *Fausta next. The star in front of this mare's name is to indicate that she is a foreign-bred—in this case, Chile. She has had two races since coming to the United States neither very impressive, though she did all right in four HdS, in Chile. And they do breed some excellent distance horses down there. But I have found it pays to play these starred horses only off their U. S. record, if any. It seems to take them a while to get acclimated. Her two races here have both been claimers. I cannot, in clear conscience, rate her as other than a claiming-class mare until she shows otherwise.

Since we've taken the time to look at her, however, it is just as well to note that she did show a three-call closing pattern in her last, which was on January 23, at Hialeah. She was seventeen lengths back at the pre-stretch call; nine and three-quarter lengths off the pace at the in-stretch call. She finished, beaten by nine and a half lengths. Not impressive, but still a closing effort. There is an indication here that she may be coming to hand. And her 1/p is positive, since she was beaten by twenty-three lengths in her previous race and by nine and a half in her last.

There is another starred horse in this race, *Djericho; but he has had nine races here in a bit over a year, all of them claimers, and no condition to recommend him in this one. We mention him because he may have come here from France with an illustrious record behind him (I don't know this) and high hopes before him that he has not lived up to.

Immediately preceding *Djericho, our roving eye catches a closing pattern for the filly, On the Quiet. Since her record brings up another kind of problem, it would be well to look at it now. First, the closing pattern. At the pre-stretch call she was ninth, fifteen lengths back; at the instretch call she was eighth, nine and three-quarter lengths off the pace; and she came on to finish fifth beaten by only three and a quarter lengths. Not a four-call pattern, but certainly a good one.

Out of curiosity, we checked her last race for 1/p only, to find that she fell at the first call and did not finish. This was a mud race at Tropical on January 12; she obviously was not hurt in the fall, as witness her strong closing race since. So we are justified in going back to her next previous race, on January 9 at Tropical, to get an 1/p comparison. She was beaten by twelve lengths in that one, so has a positive 1/p, a nine-length improvement.

Still another starred horse, *Galan, with nothing but claimers in his record, has a positive 1/p.

These three—*Fausta, On the Quiet, and *Galan—could be the principals in a limited "dutching" move.

So there is no play for us on class-condition control in the first race.

The second at Hialeah is a maiden special weight for 3-year-old fillies. Anything above this category can be basically qualified as a contender.

There are four. Foolish Question was out in an Alw at Garden State and in two AlwM at Atlantic City. Nighter's View contested two Alw, one at Tropical and one at Randall. Riverside Gal had an AlwM at Sportsman's Park. Sharp Needle ran in an AlwS at Gulfstream Park and in an Alw at Tropical.

Though Needle Sharp has the best class line, with her exposure in the AlwS, she has not raced since January 8, so is automatically dropped for being over the time limit. Foolish

Question had a closing pattern in her race on January 18, at Hialeah (time limit okay), from pre-stretch to finish, where she wound up in the three hole, beaten by eight and a half lengths. In her previous finish, at Gulfstream Park she was soundly trounced by twenty-two lengths. So she has a positive 1/p.

She definitely qualifies for play at this point, while we look at the other two contenders, both of which qualify on time limit.

However, Nighter's View lost ground steadily from first call to finish and has a negative 1/p. Ditto Riverside Gal. Neither can be given any consideration by any stretch of the imagination.

Foolish Question is the play.

The third race is a three-furlong "baby" race with a whole flock of first-time starters. We pass.

And the fourth is the one in which we qualified Grandpa David on speed conversion, remember? So we move on to the fifth stanza. This is an $8,500 claimer for 3-year-olds, going one and one-eighth miles.

Roncevalles had an allowance outing on December 21 at Tropical, which was also his last race. He is out of reach on our time limit. Jumping Bean had an allowance race at Aqueduct on October 28, 1961. Her last race was at Hialeah on January 17, which gets her under the wire on time limit. But her running pattern in the last race leaves something to be desired. It was not a really bad race, a mild giving way for each call from first to finish, to run fourth, beaten by four lengths. But coming after a win in her previous race, it fairly shouts a warning.

Close Order had three Alw races, one at Hialeah, one at Tropical, and one at Pimlico. His race on January 19 was good. While not a perfect pattern, he finished third, beaten by five and a quarter lengths, after a seventh by nine and a half at first call. We looked at this race first because his last one, on January 26, one week after the good one, was unbelievably bad. He was away last in a twelve-horse field, and was fourteen lengths behind the pace at the first call. His jockey did not persevere with him after that bad beginning, so the 1/p was definitely negative.

Since Close Order's good race (on January 19) was in an $8,500 claimer, and the bad last race was in an Alw one week later, and he is back in an $8,500 claimer, the thing looks very susiciously like a trainer's maneuver to dust Close Order off for a melon-cutting. If that was what he had in mind, he certainly scared the two-buck bettors off with that bad race. But, suspicious though we were, our class-condition control rejected him, so we had no choice but to disqualify him.

Top Card has an Alw at Hialeah on January 26, her one and only race, and it was a poor one; so we move on to look at Chicago Count. This beastie has five Alw in his class line, two of them at Hialeah and three at Aqueduct. He raced last on January 24, which qualifies him on time limit, but he backed up all the way to be beaten by twenty-one lengths—eight lengths worse than his previous beating. Chicago Count is not for us.

The next and last contender in this race is Gerald K., with two Alw at Latonia last August. His last-race pattern is an odd one. At the first call he was running eighth by five and three-quarter lengths. At the pre-stretch call he was running sixth, but by seven and a half lengths; around the bend and into the stretch for the third call, he was seventh, nine and a half lengths back of the pace. (*Note:* he has been backing up all the way to this point from a lengths-off-pace standpoint.) Now, as they drive down to the wire, his running position worsens to eighth position, but his beaten-lengths improve to six and a half. He appears to have closed three lengths in the run to the wire, while losing position from seventh to eighth.

For us, this whole race has the feeling of being out of kilter, but we finish our look-see at Gerald K. In his previous race, in which he lost ground all the way, he was beaten by seven and a quarter lengths. This gives him a three-quarter length, borderline 1/p improvement. We could qualify him, but we don't like it. And we practice what we preach: when in doubt, pass the race.

Quite frankly, we would not have risked a dime of our money on Gerald K. in that race, but since many of the inexperienced fans might not have analyzed it so carefully, and might have chosen to let the positive 1/p carry the weight, we will include this one as a play in our workout.

The sixth at Hialeah is a $10,000 claimer for 3-year-olds, going one and one-sixteenth miles.

This one is destined to be a mad scramble and it presents a new kind of problem to the fan. There are seven Alw contenders in this race: Moss Eater, with two Alw; Montedeb, with four; Shopping Center, with one; Payola, with three; By Invitation, with two Alw and three AlwM; Rash Action, with six Alw; and Nashmont, with three Alw and one AlwS. Of these, Moss Eater, Montedeb, Shopping Center, Payola and Rash Action all show positive 1/p. To make the outcome even more unpredictable, three of the noncontenders also have positive 1/p. These are Big Art, Volga, and Lady Erin—ten horses in a field of twelve definitely showing promise of winning form.

No, fellers and gals, this is not for conservative speculators like us.

The seventh at Hialeah is the feature race. It is an allowance named the Indian River Purse, a six-furlong sprint in which we will be looking for previous stakes contenders. And every one of them, of which there are six starters, has at least one stake in his class line. So we will have to look at them all.

We disqualify Vital Force, Foreign Land, Nile Melody, and Bonus because of negative 1/p and poor last-race patterns. This leaves us with Rideabout and Three M. R., both four-year-old colts.

Rideabout raced last on January 18, which is within our 15-day limit. He has one HcpS in his class line; all the rest, nine of them, are Alw. The HcpS was at Saratoga, way back last August.

He shows a fine closing pattern in his last, an Alw that he won going away by one and three-quarter lengths, and because of which he has to pick up an impost of 123 pounds today. He also won his previous race, by a head, at Tropical Park on January 8. Both of these were at today's distance and on fast strips. His 1/p is positive.

Three M. R. has one HcpS and three AlwS in his class line. His last race, an Alw on the turf course at five and a half furlongs, was on January 24 (eight days ago) and he was definitely sharp, though a little "short" in the run to the wire. The reason I say he was "definitely sharp" is because he has a virtually perfect three-race pattern, such as we gave as an example earlier in the text. I'm going to put this down so the fan can see how it looks. Since I have no small upper-case letters on my typewriter, I'm going to show the lengths and/or fractions thereof in parentheses; 1(h), for example, will read, "leading by a head."

First Call	Second Call	Third Call	Finish
1(h)	1(h)	2(h)	2(1¾)
1(1)	2(h)	2(h)	3(3)
1(h)	3(1½)	3(3)	5(12)

Here is a pattern that says this should be the time. And his 1/p (see finish positions in above example) is positive.

We have two horses sharp and ready. Both have their speed and are in condition to display it. Both have a touch of stakes class, though Three M. R.'s class line is somewhat the best, with three AlwS in addition to the one HcpS. And Three M. R.'s weight assignment of only 113 pounds means that Rideabout is being asked to spot him ten.

Still, from the viewpoint of this control system, considerable doubt exists as to who is going to beat whom. The odds, which we have learned not to trust, hand the race to Rideabout on a silver platter. He is made an odds-on favorite at 4 to 5. Bonus is second choice at 3 to 1 and Three M. R. is third choice at 4 to 1.

This does not affect our judgment, except to cause us to note that it would be unprofitable to play both Rideabout and Three M. R. to win at these odds, for we would not quite recover our investment should Rideabout win. On the other hand, the profit would be worthwhile if Three M. R. won at 4 to 1.

We decide to play them both, and rely on the 123-pound impost to slow Rideabout down enough. We would certainly not blame any student-fan for passing this, however, on our repeated admonition "When in doubt, pass the race." Nor do we feel we are leading the fan into bad habits in this case, for we have shown before that a mild form of "dutching" can at times be useful and profitable. And we plan to deal with this in more detail later in the text.

So we move on to the eighth race at Hialeah. This is the Caloosa Purse, another allowance affair and a sort of co-feature, this time at the route distance of one and one-eighth miles. The purse is a bit smaller, and the competition correspondingly less illustrous. But again, since this is an allowance, we expect our contenders to have had some stakes exposure.

There are two, Esp and Thunder Hill, each with one ScwS showing in his past performance. These, as we indicated before, do not carry much weight. We feel that they rightly belong at the very bottom of the stakes scale, for they are too often used, by trainers in doubt, as feelers to see if their juveniles may possibly have a touch of class.

Esp, a 3-year-old colt, raced last at Hialeah on January 26. He qualifies on time limit, but his running pattern was a very dismal thing to see. He never got closer than twelve lengths of the pace, and backed up in the stretch to be beaten by seventeen lengths. His 1/p is definitely negative.

Thunder Hill, on the other hand—a 3-year-old gelding who raced last on January 27 at Hialeah—shows a bit of promise. he closed from first call to the in-stretch call, only to falter by a half-length to run second, beaten by five lengths. In his race one week ago, he was beaten by eight and three-quarter lengths, so his 1/p is positive.

We qualify him with only one reservation: We would like him better if he had become a contender on something meatier than an ScwS. But this *is* within the stakes realm, so we count him a play.

Now we go into the nightcap. This is a $3,500 claimer for 4-year-olds and upward, going one and a half miles.

Only two have anything other than claimers in their class lines. One is *Plin, an Ireland-bred gelding, with one AlwS and one HcpO back in 1961. Since then, he has run in claimers somewhat cheaper than today's brand, and without much success. The other is Bespoken, with an Alw (at Belmont) under his belt and some much higher grade claimers.

By virtue of *Plin's AlwS, however, we try to qualify, or

disqualify him first, only to find that he is unraced since December 27, so he is automatically dropped from further consideration. This leaves the way open for Bespoken, with his allowance exposure at Belmont Park. And his last race was something to call special attention to.

It was remarkable, because he apparently got left at the post. At the quarter, or first call, he was twelfth in a twelve-horse field, twenty-three lengths behind the pace. At the pre-stretch call, he was ninth, nine and a half lengths back; at the in-stretch call, he was in contention, third, only two lengths away. He finished second, beaten by only one and a quarter lengths. A truly commendable performance, one that hints of considerably more class than his today's price tag would indicate.

This race was contested on January 30, two days ago, which means that his trainer had him entered for both contests, just in case, some time ago. His previous race was run on January 19. He ran fourth in that one, beaten by eight and a quarter lengths. So he has a positive 1/p improvement of seven lengths.

Bespoken is our selection. Let's have a look at our work sheet for the day.

RACE	HORSE	WIN	PLACE	SHOW
2	Foolish Question	$16.40	$6.30	$4.10
4	Grandpa David (Spd)	5.10	3.00	2.60
5	Gerald K.	...	...	...
7	{ Rideabout	...	...	2.20 }
	{ Three M. R.	10.50	7.50	3.10 }
8	Thunder Hill (entry)	...	4.90	3.20
9	Bespoken	6.50	4.40	3.60

Any complaints, anybody? Four winners out of six tries—and this *was* a rather trying day at Hialeah. We feel we really earned our winners. Some days are like that. Others, they seem to fall in your lap.

We have one more winter track to check, so let's head for California and see if we can make the Mutuel Monster cough up anything at Santa Anita. Here the racing week is five days; both Sunday and Monday are dark at Santa Anita.

We will recall that we were unable, with our speed-conversion control, to uncover a play in any of the first four races, so we'll start from scratch.

The first race is a six and a half furlong claimer for 3-year-olds bred in California. Spoon Shot, Bazooka Flash (a first-time starter), Admiralty, and Moolah Lady we pass by. We're looking for something better than claimers, remember.

Dague had an Alw outing at Bay Meadows on September 19, 1961. He raced last at Santa Anita on January 27, which is within our 15-day limit. But that is all we can say for it; it was bad from the start to finish—he was beaten by nine horses and ten lengths.

Irish Tune does not measure up as a contender since he has only claiming races in his class line. Tulips Dandy is next. She has an AlwS at Pomona, which is a county fair half-miler. She also has three Alw, one at Del Mar and two at Hollywood Park. But she is unraced since January 4, so we discard her.

Tower Bott and Encomia do not qualify as contenders, but City Babe does, with three Alw in her class line. One of these was at Tanforan and two at Agua Caliente.

In her last race, on January 18 (within our 15-day limit), she showed a lot of run for a half-mile—then faded, to be beaten by twelve lengths. In her previous race (at Tanforan), he was beaten by thirty lengths, so she does have a positive 1/p. She qualifies. Her third and fourth races back were both winning efforts, but they were in October (at Bay Meadows), so City Babe appears to be rounding to form again and has little to beat in this hassle.

Burn Early does not qualify as a contender. Bay Mystery does, with four Alw and a last outing on January 19. But she has a negative 1/p, which disqualifies her.

L. K. Drag is not a qualified contender.

Bazooka Flash, Pilaf, Girlish Gait, and Little Belina were scratched.

So, City Babe is our only qualifier and there is no decision left to us. It could be that that tightener on January 18, in which she displayed a lot of early foot, was all she needed.

The second race at Santa Anita is an allowance race for 3-year-old maidens. What we must look for in here is something better than an AlwM.

There are two. Moody has an Alw, on January 3 at Santa Anita, and qualifies on time limit, since his last was on January 19 at Santa Anita. But he has a negative 1/p, so we move on for a look at Near Paradise. This colt has an AlwS, at Bay Meadows last October, but is unraced since January 9.

We pass the race, after noting that it may be a "dutching" tool for later consideration.

The third is a "baby" race for maiden colts and geldings. Not enough line here for us to make a selection.

The fourth is an allowance race for 3-year-olds who have never won a race other than maiden or claiming. They are going six panels.

Pappa's Move shows two AlwS, but is disqualified at once on time limit. Byk had an AlwS at Hollywood Park last Spring, and has since run seven furlongs, on a slow track at Santa Anita on January 19. This was neither very good nor very bad. He lost a little ground steadily from first call to finish, to be run fourth, beaten by five lengths. His 1/p is positive, with a four and three-quarter length improvement from previous to last races.

Scan the Sky has had three AlwS exposures, but his negative 1/p says not today. Remote Control had a five-furlong race at Hollywood Park in AlwS company last May. His last race, on January 19, was good, but nevertheless it's a warning, since he won his previous race (on January 5), which looked like an easy triumph. But after setting all the pace into the stretch in the last race, he did not have enough edge left to last out the stretch-drive, where Killoqua took his measure by one and a quarter lengths. Hence a negative 1/p for Remote Control.

Lucky Uncle has a recent race and an AlwS, but a negative 1/p. Royal Arm we toss out on time limit. Turalea ditto, though he has much the best class line in the race.

Harpo appears to be in the best condition, but shows only straight allowances in his class line.

So the nod goes to Byk as the only qualifier.

This was an interesting race. Remote Control was made the even-money favorite as we expected he would be. He was a hard one to disqualify on his record, but the 1/p said no.

Let's watch the race and see what happens.

The crowd quiets to the pre-race hush. The flag goes up.

The bell rings as the gates slam open, and they're off and running.

At the start, it's Turalea taking the lead. Harpo is second, and Pappa's Move is third.

At the quarter, Remote Control is in command by one length. Pappa's Move is second by 1½ lengths. Toot The Flute is third, a head before Harpo.

Passing the half-mile pole, it's Remote Control by two lengths. Pappa's Move is second by two lengths. Byk is third a head before Harpo.

Around the turn and into the stretch, it's still Remote Control by 1½ lengths. Pappa's Move clings to second by 1½ lengths. Harpo is now third, a head before Byk.

A sixteenth out, Harpo overhauls Pappa's Move . . .then a very tired Remote Control. . . . to take command. Byk moves with him, clings to his flank in second. Lucky Uncle makes a belated bid and moves into third, ahead of Pappa's Move. Remote Control fades back to seventh.

As they drive under the wire, it's Harpo by three-quarters of a length. Byk is second, a neck better than Lucky Uncle.

Harpo, a 13 to 1 shot, paid $29.40, $12.00, and $7.20 across the board. Byk, second choice in the betting at 7 to 2, paid $6.20 to place and $5.40 to show. Remote Control was seventh.

The fifth race is another allowance, this one for fillies and mares, 4-year-olds and upward, going one and one-sixteenth miles.

Cat Call, Can't Sleep, °Narva, Paris Pike, and Bride of Egypt each show at least one HcpS in their class lines. We disqualify Can't Sleep and Paris Pike because of a negative 1/p in each case.

Cat Call raced last on January 26. She ran a strong race into the stretch, closing all the way, then hung while tired horses came back to her, so that she bettered her position without closing any additional ground in the stretch. Her 1/p was positive, however, so she stands as a qualifier.

°Narva in the same race with Cat Call (January 26) raced strongly into the stretch, then folded, to lose by seven lengths in the drive to the wire. Positive 1/p.

Bride of Egypt ran an even race in her last on January 25, in contention all the way to finish fourth, two and a half lengths behind the winner. In her previous race, she had set all the pace into the stretch, then was a bit short in the stretch run.

Her positive 1/p also testifies to her nearness to peak form. It should be noted, too, that, while she ran fourth in her last and second in her previous, she was beaten by only two and a half lengths in her last and by four and a half lengths in her previous. Just a reminder that in figuring 1/p we deal in *lengths* rather than in running-position figures.

She looks pretty good, but so do the other two, insofar as class-condition control is concerned. But we are more than slightly disturbed by the fact that *Narva, like too many of the foreigh-bred horses, does not seem able to cope with racing in the United States. In *Narva's case, she has been unable to account for a single win in twenty-three starts (see box score, in upper right-hand corner, of her past performances). Bride of Egypt, on the other hand, has won four of her starts (none recently enough to affect her ability now), and Cat Call has won two of hers.

We had not intended to introduce this win-ability gimmick until we considered the "name" handicaps, such as the Arcadia Handicap, which is the feature race today at Santa Anita. However, this seems a good place to use it to separate these three qualified HcpS contenders. Otherwise, we have three qualifiers and the odds-spread is not tempting enough to warrant "dutching" all three.

It can be readily seen that we will have to have an additional separation medium for final separation in the "name" handicaps, since for these we are already dealing with a very high grade of stakes performer, and thus cannot search out a higher type of race as a qualifying contention, as we have in the lesser events. This is where win-ability comes in, for it is true that the champion or near-champion must necessarily be a very consistent animal. His speed is taken for granted. His class is taken for granted. His ability, or will, to win races can be read directly from his box score. It is an additional proof of his inherent speed and inherent class. And, just as important, it reflects his trainer's propensity for correctly spotting him.

It is true that some of the cheaper horses, as well as the near-champs, have good consistency records, but consistency alone does not make a horse a champion. The cheap horse has consistency because his trainer keeps him spotted at his own class-level. So when we are dealing with "name" handicap racers, we are dealing with them at *their* level.

If I seem to digress, or get slightly ahead of the seventh race, it is because, having isolated three HcpS competitors and assuming from this that we are dealing with stakes-level racers who need further separation, we may be able to separate this trio by win-ability.

Please understand that win-ability can at no time be considered a substitute for condition. For it is just as true that a horse to be consistent must be in condition as it was true that it was a necessary part of his ability to display speed or class.

We have already satisfied ourselves that each of this trio has recent evidence of approaching peak form. And of these three in-condition horses, Bride of Egypt shows a definite superiority in win-ability. Notice that we did not bother with figuring percentage of consistency, which is the more popular way of doing it, but simply used the superior number of wins shown in the box score.

On this separation basis, we qualify Bride of Egypt for play.

The sixth race at Santa Anita is a six-furlong, $15,000 claimer for 4-year-olds and upward. There are twelve starters and, as might be expected in a high-grade claimer, all, at one time or another, have been exposed to a higher grade of race. We can reduce our work somewhat, by eliminating those who have been risked for a claiming price at some time in the past, on the theory that a trainer who has never risked losing his horse in a claiming race thinks more highly of him than a trainer who has taken this risk.

This, we feel, is a logical supposition.

So we eliminate Bragg Hill, Garden Fresh, and Perfect Hostess. This still leaves us with nine contenders, so we'll see how many we can dispose of on the time limit.

We disqualify three more: Long Ears, Comeflywithme, and Inoorpapa, who have not raced within our 15-day limit.

We get rid of three more on negative 1/p. Noor's Story, Dimity, and Wise June fall by the wayside.

We have three left: Gun Box, Daiichi, and Sweet Lilly.

Gun Box, in her last race, on January 25 at Santa Anita, after an alert beginning dropped back to Seventh at the second call, three and three-quarter lengths off the pace. At the in-stretch call, she was still seventh, three and three-quarter lengths back. Then, under belated pressure, she closed to fifth, three and a quarter lengths behind the winner as they came under the wire. We have seen better patterns, but she did have something left at the end. And since she was beaten by five and a quarter lengths in her previous race (also at Santa Anita, on January 9), she has a positive 1/p.

Daiichi raced last at Santa Anita on January 18, which qualifies her on time limit, and though she did not show a perfect closing pattern, it was a strong race. She was second at the first call, only a head off the pace; at the second call, she was still running second by a head; into the stretch she took command by a half-length and won by three-quarters of a length. This after having been long rested since August, after she finished second at Arlington Park, beaten by one and a half lengths. So she has a positive 1/p.

Sweet Lilly, off her January 18 race at Santa Anita, shows us a perfect closing pattern. She was ninth, five and three-quarter lengths back of the pace at the first call; sixth, four and a quarter lengths back at the pre-stretch call; and fourth by three and a half lengths at the in-stretch call. She finished second, beaten by only three-quarters of a length. In her previous race (on December 28 at Santa Anita), she was beaten by five and a quarter lengths. So here again we have a positive 1/p.

This has been an unusually tough race to try to analyze. And once we do get it boiled down to three horses—or, rather, two mares and a filly—we find they are all qualified on recent condition.

We have run some risks to get this far, sacrificing some of our percentage edge in an effort to whittle the field to where it can be dealt with—only to be confronted with a three-way tie. And the odds are not particularly inviting for a three-horse "dutch."

After all our work, we are still confronted by considerable doubt. I will not say these qualifiers cannot be separated, but I do not think the student-fan should attempt it. Not yet. For now, I think we should agree there is still considerable doubt, and pass the race.

Oh! So you think I'm hedging—ducking out of a difficult situation? How would I, personally, separate these three tied lady-horses?

All right! First, I would eliminate Sweet Lilly—and I can almost hear you gasp, because she is the one with the perfect closing pattern, which we have learned to regard highly. *But,* she is also a filly, and it is one of my personal foibles that I will not back a filly against a mare if they figure close. A filly, even a 4-year-old filly, is still flighty and undependable.

So, despite your gasps and probable frowns of disapproval, I stick to my guns. Sweet Lilly must be dropped.

So now we still have two mares to deal with. No, I'm not going to fudge and say that we can now afford to play both, since Sweet Lilly was the short-priced one.

I'm going to use the axe on Daiichi. Why? She also has a better closing pattern than the other mare, Gun Box. You're right, of course, but she set up this pattern in her very first outing after a six-month layoff. In the first place, I'm wondering why a good one like her has been eating her oats instead of earning them for six long months. In the second place, it's rare that a beastie will win at first asking after a long rest. The trainer will not ask for this the first time out, as a rule, but will expect to give the horse an easy trial to tighten him up for a win later. But this trainer did bring Daiichi out and let her win at first asking. And she was under pressure from first call to finish. For a horse not tightened up by recent racing, she is almost certain to have given her all to win that one. It is my personal opinion that she will be unable to win another in the foreseeable future, in spite of her 1/p. In short, I don't think she has anything left at this time.

Gun Box, I think we will all agree, was not used up in her last race. She would be my choice—as long as you have forced me to stick my neck out—as the one most likely to give me a real run for my money. On top of this, there is a jockey switch from Harmatz to Willie Shoemaker, with which I find no fault at all.

Gun Box took the lead at the first call and never relinquished it, coasting in to a two and three-quarter length win.

Daiichi was third by half a length at the first call, then faded to fifth, to eighth, and finished ninth, beaten by eight or nine lengths.

Sweet Lilly never raised a gallop.

The race was still no play on the doubtful premise for the student-fan. Later, when you have developed some facility in handling these various controls, you will see these "hidden" things for yourself. You will form your own selecting habits. You will *know* when you have the edge with you.

So now we're ready to look at the Arcadia Handicap. Notable II has been scratched. We will get rid of one more by picking a sure loser. This is Odd Fellow, who has one HcpO and one Alw in his past performance, all the rest being claimers. He simply doesn't belong in this kind of company. Since all the rest are well studded with HcpS events and must be presumed to be *ready* for a purse of this size, which is $25,000 added, we will call on win-ability to isolate the most probable winner for us. We are not too surprised to see that this puts us on the second-highest impost of the field—Art Market, with nine wins in his box score and 120 pounds assigned. Oink is top weight, with 124 pounds, and is second-best on win-ability, with eight in his box score.

We frequently pass these "big ones" when at the racing wars. Too often they are unfigurable by normal means, or else they're a vehicle for a current hotshot to display his wares at some very short price. But in this one, our choice is being allowed to go to the post at 7 to 1, while everybody chunks it in on Oink, who has been beaten down to 6 to 5.

So, when we play the "name" handicaps at all, we assume they are all ready, and that they are entered to shoot the works for the large end of the purse. Our edge is the win-ability factor, which in this case points up Art Market.

In the eighth at Santa Anita, which is a claiming race for 4-year-olds and upward, going one and one-sixteenth miles, we go back to our class-condition control.

Vegas Bandit shows an HcpS at Pomona, which, as we pointed out before, is a county fair half-miler. The best we can say for a stake at this bullring is that it must be held suspect in the quality department. In any case, this gelding backed up from start to finish in his last race (on January 24 at Santa Anita) and finished tenth, beaten by twenty-nine lengths. His 1/p is negative.

Our next contender, Kaycee's Wonder, shows two HcpS at Exhibition Park last July and August and five HcpO, all at the same track. When he moved to Tanforan, he was sent out in the claiming class, and his one outing at Santa Anita (on January 23) was also a claimer. His 1/p is negative.

Flamestone has two Alw races, one at Belmont and one at Saratoga, neither held suspect, but he is unraced since November 11, 1961, at Aqueduct. A nonqualifier.

Sir Leveler has one Alw at Del Mar and one at Hollywood Park. He raced last on January 26 at Santa Anita, but he also has a negative 1/p. Brian Hickey has an assortment of HcpS and HcpO at Exhibition Park, and just squeezes by on time limit off his race at Santa Anita on January 17, but he also has a negative 1/p, so we pass the nightcap.

Here's our work sheet for the day at Santa Anita:

1	City Babe	$13.20	$7.80	$5.60
4	Byk	. . .	6.20	5.40
5	Bride of Egypt	5.60	3.80	3.20
7	Art Market	16.40	5.60	4.00

So at Santa Anita also, the Mutuel Monster will disgorge if properly persuaded.

CHAPTER NINE   *Sprints vs. Routes*

As a change of pace, and by way of a refresher, now that we are about to leave winter racing for the nonce and pick up our work at the three spring tracks, a question occurs to us that might be giving some of you pause.

Since our first control was speed conversion, some of you may be wondering why we applied this only to sprint distances in the early races.

In the first place, in sprint races—and most particularly cheap sprint races—speed, or lack of it, is about the only tangible commodity we are able to figure. It gives us a hint of any small spark of class a cheap horse may have. In the second place, a sprint race is a speed race. A route race, though there must be speed-ability in order to win, is more often the result of clever rating by a jockey who is a superior judge of pace.

In the cheap sprint race, then, it is a slam-bang, helter-skelter scamper from gate to wire. There is little time, or opportunity, to try to "rate" a horse. In fact, we have it from no less an authority than Eddie Arcaro, that "it's impossible to rate a cheap horse."

His contention was that with a cheap horse the jockey just went along for the ride. If the hide happened to be fast enough to beat this bunch, then you rode a winner. If he wasn't, you didn't.

This is probably an oversimplification, but it brings out the point I was making, that we have little to work with in a cheap sprint but speed—relative speed, that is, since a cheap sprinter is not really a very speedy beastie. But if he happens to be a little faster basically than the hides he's competing against—and if his condition factor is right, of course—we can back him with just as much confidence as we could a better grade horse in a better grade race.

Then, as we consider the route races, while there must be a certain speed-ability, it is more a question of stamina, which in itself is an indication of class. For instance, a horse that has shown little speed-ability in sprint races might do quite well, in his class-level, in the longer races, simply because he does not tire as fast. He has more stamina, when in condition, than his faster cousin who lacks the strength and stamina to "run all day." He will still not set any speed records. By our Speed Standards charts, he may still show no faster ratings than he did when sprinting. The difference is in his stamina, his ability to carry his plodding progress well beyond the sprint distances without the rapid rate of slow-down common to the sprinter who cannot carry his speed beyond a certain sprint distance.

This relatively faster sprinter, then, when asked to go the route distances, will turn in much slower standard ratings than the plodder who can't get close to him in the sprint distances.

As we go on up the class ladder, we begin to find horses with both blazing speed and stamina. These are the cream. Of this kind of stuff is the champion made.

This, of course, is elementary. But it's amazing how few fans ever consider it in his light. To them, a horse is a horse. Yet these same fans, presumably, would not expect a top hundred-yard-dash man, among human athletes, to be able to keep up with a four-minute-miler—or vice versa. The decathlon champ can do most of the required atheltic feats better than any of his contemporaries—that's why he is crowned decathlon champion —but you can bet there is still some one event that he does best.

As we moved away from the cheap sprinters, we no longer belabored speed because we no longer had to limit ourselves. The speed is there. It increases automatically with the raising of the class of competition. We take it for granted. But there is no reason why we cannot call on it again at any time in a difficult separation. It might well tell us if this is the best distance for one of our contenders.

While we try to avoid splitting hairs, sometimes there will be a worthwhile preference in speed-ability *at this distance* that would not be apparent except by clinical speed comparison. And there will be times when neither hoss has been raced at exactly today's distance, but both have recently raced at a common distance, one close enough to today's distance to be indicative so that we can make a profitable comparison at that common distance.

We will attempt to point this up by specific examples as we go on with our work.

So now we find ourselves back at Gulfstream Park, at Hallandale, Florida, on April 2, 1962. This, incidentally, is Blue Monday, and Gulfstream is on the final weeks of its meeting. Already, some of the stables have shipped north for the opening of the spring campaign. Though this is the tag end of a long Florida winter of racing, it is also the beginning of spring racing

Personally, in April you can never pry me away from Gulfstream—not until the last race is run. The illusion that the northern pastures are greener is just that—an illusion.

So let's take up our customary stand, and see how the exodus has affected the racing scene at Gulfstream, if at all.

In the first race, we will recall, we had a speed-conversion selection, El Misterio, so we move on to the second race.

This was a seven-furlong affair for 3-year-old maidens under allowance conditions, so we will look for our contenders above this category. We may also recall that we couldn't work this one on speed conversion because too few had been raced at this distance.

King's Highway was raced at Gulfstream Park on March 27 in an AlwM, so qualifies on time limit. Aside from two AlwM, this gelding has been raced in eight maiden special weights (Md Sp Wt), but his 1/p is negative.

Nettie's Gal has two straight Alw races among her past performances and has raced recently enough, but her 1/p is neutral (8/8).

By Invitation also has two straight Alw and was recently raced, but after a very promising race on March 20, which he was obviously trying very hard to win, backed up in his race on March 27, creating a negative 1/p.

Bueno Road has two AlwM in his past performances. That's all. This is the same classification as today's race.

Easy Story is unraced since March 1 at Hialeah, so is disqualified on time limit.

Bianco Mano raced at 7 panels on March 27 at Gulfstream, and closed resolutely in the stretch to be third, beaten by only two lengths. But she was beaten by only two and a quarter lengths in her previous race; thus she cannot be said to have a positive 1/p.

Saquestte raced on March 20 at GP and has one Alw in her class line. In both her last two races, we note that she broke tardily and backed up all the way to the finish line, to be beaten by nineteen lengths in her last race and by twenty-seven in her previous, thus creating a positive 1/p of 19/27. Wow! And yet an 1/p of these proportions *could* mean something. Supposing Saquestte was pitched way over her head in both those races and is today facing the kind of speed that she can conceivably cope with. Even such a far-out fringe 1/p as hers does indicate a bit of improvement. So, instead of summarily tossing her out, we'll go back to her after seeing what other contenders we have, if any.

Tudor Echo could be qualified as a contender and was raced recently, but has a negative 1/p (10/7¼).

Star Piper was raced on March 20. Okay on the time limit. He has one A1wM and two Md Sp Wt. His last race is not a perfect pattern, but he may have had a rough trip. He was fourth by three lengths at the first call; fourth by five and a half at the second call; then challenged to get up to third only half a length off the pace. He was a little short from his effort in the run to the wire, finishing third, beaten by one and a half lengths. Yes, there is definite evidence of winning form there, and the positive 1/p (1½/9½) further verifies this.

But what about Saquestte? She qualified on 1/p too. Actually, the vast difference in the two patterns, and the equally noticeable difference in the two 1/ps, would be sufficient justification for dropping Saquestte and giving the final nod to Star Piper. Our conscience would be clear if we did this, but since we were discussing speed as an added separation medium a few paragraphs back, let's see what it can do for us here. After all, there is a remote chance that those two races in which Saquestte looked bad might have been unusually fast, thus making her converted speed-rating comparable to Star Piper's.

Neither of these hides has been out at today's distance, but both have travelled six furlongs recently. Star Piper maneuvered this distance one and a half lengths behind Khanhai, who won it in 1:12, which is standard. Star Piper, then, gets a plus one and a half standard rating, for this was a fast strip.

Saquestte competed in this same race, so had a plus 19. These two are seventeen and a half lengths apart on speed. Sure, we could have pointed this out earlier, and doubtless some of you sharp-eyed fans saw it, but we wanted an excuse to demonstrate the use of speed comparison as a separation medium—even in a race where we were previously forced to reject speed as a selection factor.

This reminds me a little of a mathematics professor I studied (?) under, more years ago than I care to admit, at the New Mexico School of Mines, where I was matriculating in mining engineering. This man was a genius in mathematics and, I'm sure, regarded me as something considerably less than that.

The subject was calculus. Professor Reece spent thirty minutes of the hour-long torture proving, by long and ghastly differential calculus formulae, that a certain thing was true. Then in the final half-hour, using a different set of formulae, he proved that it was untrue.

So, while we could not select Star Piper on speed conversion when applying our first control, we now use speed to separate him from Saquestte, and thereby to qualify him for play.

The third race was at five furlongs, a claiming race for 2-year-old maidens.

We find two contenders who also have positive 1/p. Since these two do not have a common distance on which to base a speed separation, we will have to do the job on visual condition, if at all.

Trimette had a good closing pattern from pre-stretch to finish, closing three lengths in the stretch to finish fourth, beaten by less than one length. This was at five furlongs. In his previous race, a three-furlong straightaway, he also closed strongly, but was beaten by nine and a quarter lengths. His 1/p is positive and he qualifies on our recentness requirement.

Harriet's Comet, the other contender, has raced three times at three furlongs, the last one on March 27 at Gulfstream. He closed in both his last two races (only two calls shown in these short races). He was seventh, eight lengths off the pace at the in-stretch call, and finished seventh, beaten by seven and a quarter lengths. In his previous race, he was running eight, eleven lengths back, at the in-stretch call and finished seventh, beaten by eight and a quarter lengths. So he, too has a positive 1/p, though not as healthy a one as Trimette's.

The student-fan could not be blamed if he passed this one as doubtful, or elected to play both, since the odds would support this. Trimette went to the post at 6 to 1 and Harriet's Comet at 4 to 1.

However, let's look at this a bit further. There is a jockey switch on Trimette, from Broussard to Boulmetis. Burr has the boot again today on Harriet's Comet. Not much for us there.

Personally, I would doubtless evoke my distrust of fillies (Trimette) and decide in favor of the colt (Harriet's Comet), if it were not for one thing. Harriet's Comet has raced only on the straightaway. He has not yet been asked to race around turns, at least not in competition, and he could have trouble negotiating two of them today in this five-furlong hassle. Trimette, on the other hand, raced well at five furlongs, and apparently managed the turns like a little lady.

Since the one thing tends to cancel out the other, we would either have to pass—or play them both. And since there is little else in the race to give us pause, my decision would be to play them both. I would still blame no fan who elected to pass.

The fourth race at Gulfstream was a claiming waltz for 3-year-olds, going one and one-sixteenth miles.

Loveable John has a loveable closing pattern in his last race, which was here at GP, and a positive 1/p. Unfortunately, he is unraced since March 12, and has nothing higher than claimers in his past performance.

Col. Music has a small claim on fame with an outing in the Gulfstream Park Dinner Stakes a year ago. And he raced here on March 29, which brings him into contention on time limit. His last race pattern was not bad. Neither was it good, for he faded steadily from first call to finish. He was on the pace by a head at the first call; second by two at the pre-stretch call; still second, but four lengths away at the in-stretch call; and finished fourth, beaten by four and a half lengths. No, he is not staling off from a recent win. He hasn't won since last May, at Washington Park. And there is some indication of condition, of form, in that last race. Maybe Col. Music just doesn't possess enough "lick" to keep up. In the previous race—though he faded in that one too, and finished sixth, beaten by five and three-quarter lengths—it does give him a positive 1/p. So we hold him in abeyance while we check out the rest of them.

Plamor Bill is not a contender. He has nothing but claiming races in his past performances.

Absconder had an outing in an A1w at Gulfstream in his previous race, and since he raced last here, on March 28, he also qualifies on time limit. He won this one going away by three lengths, adding a full length to a good in-stretch lead of two lengths. He appears to have won this easily, but in this case it's an easy thing to verify. This last race was at one and one-sixteenth miles, and his standard rating for this effort was a plus 17—a truly leisurely trip, since his best rating at this distance is plus 5. We certainly have nothing to fear from a hide who won in slower time than he is capable of, and we have good reason to expect him to improve on this effort today. In the allowance race, he was beaten by seven and a half lengths, so his positive 1/p shows a ten-length improvement.

Commonish is our next possible contender, with two allowances—one at Keenland and one at Tropical. But the last one (he won his last two) was contested on March 13, which is a little too far back for us.

Hafiz, Jr., I suppose, could be brought into the contender ranks by virtue of his outing (last race) in an A1wM. He did not win that one either, so is still a maiden, and it just doesn't make good sense to qualify a maiden against horses that have already won three and four races. Neither would it make good sense to ignore him entirely simply because he is still a maiden. His connections just might have found a soft spot to drop him into. We find that Hafiz, Jr., actually did win a race on March 10, but was disqualified and placed second, thus perpetuating his maiden status.

This hide turned in a good pattern in his last, closing strongly from the pre-stretch call to the finish where he was beaten off by three lengths, while closing six and a half in the run to the wire. Yep, this beastie has a bit of condition to his credit. And to substantiate it, his 1/p is positive. But he is no great shakes as a performer, and his record suffers considerably when placed alongside that of Absconder's last race. In Absconder, we have a winner-sharp horse who was definitely not used up in that easy win. He should come back with another win in this race, though we cannot expect him to have such an easy thing of it this time. He will have to show marked improvement over his last race, which we have every reason to assume he will.

This is an interesting race. Let's watch them run.

This being a mile and a sixteenth, the start will be right in front of the stands. The pre-race hush falls on the crowd.

They're all in the gate. The flag goes up. The bell jangles—and the gates slam open. They're off and splashing in the sloppy footing.

At the start, it's Tolowa taking the lead. Col. Music is second. And Commonish.

Around the Clubhouse turn it's Col. Music, trying for a runaway by eight lengths. Tolowa is second by two lengths before Commonish. Hafiz, Jr., is fourth. Absconder is last.

At the half, Col. Music is still leading by eight lengths. Apparently Jockey Blum, understanding Col. Music's weakness in the stretch, is trying to hold him so far in front that the others won't be able to catch up when the real racing starts. Tolowa holds onto second place, one and a half lengths before Hafiz, Jr. Absconder is still trailing.

At the three-quarters call, Col. Music is still in command, but the pace is beginning to tell on him. His margin has now been reduced to one length. Hafiz, Jr., has now taken over from Tolowa and is running second. Absconder has begun his move and is now fourth.

Into the stretch, it's Hafiz, Jr., by one length. And here comes Absconder. He's third. He's second. Col. Music is now third and Tolowa fourth.

One sixteenth out, Absconder looks Hafiz, Jr., in the eye. Both horses are being hard-driven. Then Absconder moves ahead, and as they go under the wire he has the best of it by a half-length. Hafiz, Jr., is second. Col. Music saved the show.

So the maiden we nearly discarded out of hand came very close to stealing the race, forcing Absconder to extend himself to the very limit—in fact, to a new best-time for this distance. And the dear, wonderful betting public was looking the other way. Absconder paid $14.20, $7.70, and $4.40 across the board.

The fifth at GP was a seven-furlong waltz for 4-year-olds and upward, a claimer for a $9,000 price tag. There were eight starters after Wishing Bone was declared out.

Atomic Jet and Doc Wal we discard because they show

nothing but claimers in their past performances. Tudor Link is dropped on time limit, since he was unraced since February 24 at Hialeah.

Ohio Ann, a five-year-old mare, has two starter handicaps in her class line, both at Tropical Park. Her last race, on March 19 at Gulfstream (still within the time limit) showed a resonably sharp effort, though not a perfect pattern. She was leading by a half-length at the first call; second by a head at the pre-stretch call; fourth by two and a quarter lengths into the stretch. She then showed her edge by coming again to finish third, beaten by only three parts of a length. In her previous race, she faded a bit from pre-stretch to finish to be beaten eight and a half lengths. So her 1/p is positive.

Brave Spartan, with an A1w on March 6 at GP, and whose last race was on March 27, qualifies both on time limit and better-than-claimer quality, or at least on quality by association. He won the March 27 caper by one and three-quarter lengths going away. But he was also leading (half a length) at the in-stretch call, so his margin does not indicate an easy win. Let's see if speed will tell us whether it was easy or not.

This race was at six furlongs on a good track, and Brave Spartan earned a minus eight (−8) for his winning effort. Running down his past performance line, we find a six-furlong race at Woodbine (Canada), in which this colt set up a best-time of minus eighteen (−18). Both these efforts hint at something more than a mere touch of class. And Brave Spartan won that last one quite easily—indeed, a full two seconds slower than his best. His pattern was an excellent closing one from start to finish. And his previous one, in which he was beaten by only three-quarters of a length, was definitely another sharp effort. So Brave Spartan also brings us a positive 1/p.

Draper we discard because of a negative 1/p. Brandy Sea, while he showed a mildly positive 1/p, faded from pre-stretch to finish in his last race (on March 20) and so cannot be seriously considered against such a record as Brave Spartan's. Besides, his record shows a decided preference for route distances, though he did show one strong six-furlong race at Tropical last December.

Another time for Brandy Sea, for he's a pretty fair sort and might be good for cakes and coffee at another contest.

Arc Light goes into the discard on time limit.

So there is really no indecision about this one. We could not bet against Brave Spartan in this race. In fact, he looks so good that even his 4 to 5 odds-on price does not constitute an underlay. So we take him.

The sixth race is another claimer, this time at one mile on the turf course, conditioned for 3-year-olds.

This, fellers and gals, shapes up as a stinkeroo. Not that our control system will not isolate a play. It will. But because of the finagling these horses have been subject to, and the borderline time-limit element, we hold the whole race suspect. For instance, of the eight starters (Pinsetter was scratched), four are a bit under the time limit and four a bit over. But the real reason this race smells is the manner in which these horses have been shifted around in class-level.

Look at Big Art. He won at $8,500 claimer at Hialeah, and is brought right back (at Gulfstream) on March 16 in a $14,000 claimer. He is being sent out for an $11,000 price tag today. Sporty Tipper was out in a $10,000 claimer on March 3 at Hialeah, then was sent back in a $15,000 claimer on March 10. He goes for a $12,000 tag today.

Do-Pak was out in a $4,500 claimer on March 9, then was sent back in a 12,000 claimer on March 16, and is wearing the same size price tag today.

It's true that I warned you early in the text that we would not indulge in the idiocy of claiming price manipulations, and we will not, but this sort of thing makes me lose patience. In each case, the horse won its previous start, so we would expect a minimum raise in claiming tag, but this sort of thing is ridiculous—from $8,500 up to $14,000 down to $11,000. Who does this trainer think he's kidding?

Of course, this kind of analysis is beyond the scope of our control system, but as you gain experience and learn to observe more and more the maneuverings and machinations of one stable trying to outsmart another, you will, I hope, reject this sort of race out of hand.

But I digress, except to point up that even the best of control systems can be improved by a little common horse-sense observation. I just couldn't let it get by without calling your attention to the fact that to experienced eyes the race looks like a booby trap. So now we'll go on with this, strictly according to our class-condition control.

Big Art is just over the line on time limit and shows nothing but claimers in his class line. Sporty Tipper and Dor-Pak are discarded for the same reason.

Labelled, out on March 22, gets in on time limit, and is a possible contender by virtue of three A1w and two A1wS in his class line. But he won his race on March 15th impressively, only to warn us in his last that he left his best race on the track on March 15. He set all the pace in his last race, but he didn't have enough edge left in the run to the wire and finished second, beaten by three parts of a length. Thus he has a negative 1/p.

Nodarsia goes down on time limit. Roster gets in off his March 22 race at Gulfstream, and he has three A1w in his class line. His last race was a good example of a closing effort from start to finish—from tenth, thirteen lengths off the pace in his first call, to finish fourth, beaten by four and a quarter lengths. This looks good, and would be good if we did not already have our tongue in cheek about the race itself. Roster was beaten by fifteen lengths in his previous race, so shows us a positive 1/p Under our control system, he is definitely a qualifier.

Larsa is discarded on time limit. Silver Bloom has a negative 1/p.

There are only two horses in the race with closing edge: Roster, whom we have already qualified, and Big Art, who was dropped for being just under the line on time limit and because he showed only claimers in his class line.

Because he did show improvement, in spite of being sent in way over his head in that $14,000 claimer, he piques our interest, mainly because his trainer apparently tried so hard to cover the fact that Big Art had retained his sharp edge after winning his previous race. In that last race, Big Art was fourth, eight lengths off the pace at the first call; at the pre-stretch call, he was still eighth, but only three and three-quarter lengths back; then he seemed to run into traffic trouble, for he lost ten lengths from pre-stretch to in-stretch; then came on again to close two lengths in the run to the wire. This, presumably, took some doing against $14,000 horses. So Big Art was still a sharp horse after his winning race, and was certainly not hard-used in that last one.

I am not trying to make a case for Big Art, nor questioning his trainer's right to indulge in whatever tactics he might see fit to try to win another race at good odds. But it does help to explain how Big Art beat Roster, and is in keeping with our contention that there is *a reason* for everything that happens in racing.

The seventh race at Gulfstream was an allowance at one mile over the turf course (maiden, claiming, optional, and starter races not considered). And for horses who've not won two races other than maiden. This is not a very promising vehicle for the feature race of the day, but let's take a look. It may be better than the conditions would indicate. Chances ✔ are, though, that the conditions were dictated by the fact that many of the better horses have already left to get acclimated for the spring racing in the North.

We must look for stakes contention in here.

Get Lucky shows four handicap stakes in his class line, but he's been unraced since March 13 so we reject him.

Count Hash was raced on March 27 in an A1w and turned in a strong effort, but shows no stakes outings in his class line.

Deton was raced on March 24 and shows one HcpS, his last at GP, but he backed up all the way in this one, and his previous races are not indicative of approaching sharp form, though it may have been the too classy competition in that last one that made him look bad. In any case, he has a negative 1/p, so we discard him. He was subsequently scratched, in any case.

Bigfork showed evidence of condition in his last race pattern on March 24, but may have left his best effort on the track in trying to win that one, which the *Telegraph* called out as the Donn H, and which appeared as an HcpS in the *Form*. In any case, his 1/p is negative. Wise Command was also out in the Donn H, but turned in a very dismal effort, and has a negative 1/p. Swift Sands, though he turned in a promising effort in his last on March 25 (an A1w), shows no stakes efforts in his class line. He has a positive 1/p.

So we have no qualifier in this race. We do have two horses that look good on the condition factor—Count Hash and Swift Sands—both substantiated by positive 1/p, but neither qualifies on stakes contention.

The eighth is a claimer for 4-year-olds and upward, going six furlongs. There are five qualified contenders: Cyclobob, Arstar, Asado, Count Rose, and Ray H. K. Of these, only Count Rose shows a closing pattern and a positive 1/p. He is our qualifier. There is nothing new in the way of problems in this race, so there would be little point in laboring it. While I want you to have the benefit of as much horse-to-horse analysis as I am able to give you, there is little point in tiring you with needless repetition.

The ninth, the nightcap here at Gulfstream, is a cheap claimer for 4-year-olds and upward, who are being asked to run one and one-sixteenth miles.

Eclair II has two starter Hcp, both at Aqueduct, way back last October and November (1961). This eight-year-old horse raced last on March 29 and faded steadily from the pre-stretch call to finish, but he turned in a positive 1/p.

Proud Stepper has one Alw exposure and one starter Hcp. His last race was weak, backing up all the way from the pre-stretch call, to be beaten by nineteen lengths. Even so, this race was not as bad as his previous one, so he has a lopsided 1/p (19/25). This hardly sends us, but there is some small hint in it, so we record it.

Antiquity, still a maiden, has some Md Sp Wt races in his class line beside the cheap claimers, and his last race shows evidence of approaching form, plus a positive 1/p, which forces us to consider him.

Gray's Blue Man shows a bad last-race pattern and a negative 1/p.

Lady Susan, a filly with another lopsided though positive 1/p, has only claimers in her class line.

Cute Tomata shows a mild fade all the way in her last race, but a positive 1/p. However, she shows no claim to contention with only claimers in her class line.

So, we will pass this race on to those desperate characters who are trying to get out of the barrel for the day.

Our work sheet for April 2, 1962, at Gulfstream Park, follows:

RACE	HORSE	WIN	PLACE	SHOW
1	El Misterio (spd)	$6.50	$4.00	$2.80
2	Star Piper	6.80	4.10	2.80
3	Trimette	14.80	8.80	5.10
	Harriet's Comet	. . .	6.40	4.50
4	Absconder	14.20	7.70	4.40
5	Brave Spartan	3.90	2.90	2.70
6	Roster	. . .	. . .	5.20
8	Count Rose	. . .	7.70	5.60

So we had five winning races and two horses that ran in the money. A good and profitable day.

Incidentally, the nightcap was won by Lady Susan, one of our two with far-out fringe 1/p's. And she paid $67.10. She may have gotten a few of our desperate friends out of the barrel. But we did not need her. Certainly our control does not permit us to gamble on this sort of scramble.

CHAPTER TEN

Laurel Park

Since our control complex handled the changing scene satisfactorily at Gulfstream Park, let's journey up to Laurel Park, Maryland, on our million-dollar magic carpet and see what new problems, if any, arise at this brand new spring meeting.

Many of these horses will have vanned to Laurel from Pimlico and Bowie. Pimlico, in recent years, has been running a late fall meeting—so late, in fact, that it has been overlapping into the winter months, as late as December, when snow and other inclement weather does not force closing down. And Bowie, by crowding the early spring racing, has also run into snow conditions and been forced to cancel. Neither track could really be classed as a legitimate winter operation, yet both overlap so far into this cold and blustery season that one wonders at their audacity. Frankly, I'll take my winter racing where the breezes are more balmy, where snow is something one sees in picture postcards from friends up north.

That's just one of the nice features about making one's million from racing. You don't *have* to live in frigid climates because your livelihood is there. That's right. I'm a tropical tramp at heart. I'm quite content to leave the snow and ice to the polar bears and Eskimos. In fact, April in the north is kind of crowding things for me.

So let's look at the first race at Laurel, on April 2, 1962. This was the race in which Harold Weissman was put over—remember? A maiden claimer for 3-year-olds, going six panels.

There is nothing in here for us. Harold Weissman had an allowance race at Garden State Park in October of 1961, but was unraced since November so could not be considered on time limit. Lord Patrick, Veralan, and Mac's Request had raced within the time limit. Likewise, Hidare. We might have stretched a point and qualified Veralan off her Md Sp Wt at Bowie on February 23, but she is both a filly and a maiden, and we do not feel impelled to stretch any points under such circumstances. We fall back on the "when in doubt, pass the race" loophole.

The second race is a six-furlong affair for 4-year-olds and upwards. It's a claimer with eleven starters, after scratches.

Cartridge has a whole flock of Alw and Md Sp Wt and only one cheap claimer in his past performances, but was raced last on November 8, 1961. He is discarded.

Helen's Joy shows an Alw at Charles Town (W. Va.) last December and she raced at Bowie on March 19. But she won her race at Bowie on March 13 and left her best race on the track there. Her negative 1/p eliminates her for us.

Dark Waters has three Alw, likewise at Charles Town, and raced at Bowie on March 20, but backed up in this one like he was running the wrong way. A reverse last-race pattern and a negative 1/p, disqualifies him for us.

Miss Houston won her last at Bowie on March 26. She took this one wire to wire, and had opened up an impressive eight-length lead by the time she passed under the wire. This was at five and a half furlongs, ten lengths faster than she had ever gone the distance before—or any distance for that matter. Since there is absolutely no sense in winning any race by that many lengths—and we'll bet Jockey McKee got a dressing down for doing it—it may not have been won as easily as it appears to have been. That is, there can be no question that she won the race by eight lengths, but she must have been under a drive to exceed her former best-time by ten lengths. It is quite possible she had the bit in her teeth and McKee could not restrain her, but it's our belief that she used herself up, needlessly, in that March 26 race, and will not be able to duplicate the effort today. So, in spite of the fact that she has an A1w at Charles Town (a strong race in her last) and qualifies on time limit, we would pass the race rather than qualify her for play. In short, it may prove difficult to bet against such capabilities (after we have checked the balance of the race), but we certainly would not want to risk our money on Miss Houston. On the face of it, she appears to be an outstanding play, but after analysis she is far from a sound investment, and we hope we are creating a determination in all of you not to accept things at face value. That's why we have been going to such pains to point up, and elaborate on, these special problems as they occur. As we said earlier, it's an integral part of our job, not only to try to qualify a play in a given race but also to search out the reasons, if any, to disqualify one—or at least to balance defects against favorable points before making our final decision. Every loser we avoid is money in our pockets, and we cannot afford to overlook anything in our quest for a million dollars.

So, Miss Houston qualifies beautifully on the face of her *apparent* easy-win, but it leaves us with a great big doubt after we analyze it. We hold her in abeyance until we've checked the rest of the race.

Debate, a 5-year-old horse, closed well in his last race at Bowie on March 24 and has a positive 1/p. But he shows nothing but claimers in his class line.

School Caper, a 4-year-old gelding, shows six A1w and raced

on March 26 at Bowie, but he backed up all the way from first call to finish to turn in a negative 1/p. He is definitely not sharp by our standards.

Star Velvet raced on March 26, but turned in an expected weak effort after a neck-win on March 13. His 1/p is, of course, negative.

Toy Pebble's last race was poor. He backed up more at each call from first to finish, and was beaten by eleven lengths. He is a very doubtful quantity in spite of an outside-fringe positive 1/p (11/16). He's not for us.

Sea Trend goes into the discard on time limit, being unraced since December. Grand Opera was beaten nine lengths after an impressive win, warning us off. Finkie had three good races in a row at Bowie, but his last one was a second by a neck after a win by a neck. He seems to be a game sort, but he gives us a clear enough warning.

So we still have only Miss Houston as a qualifier on figures. And we still have our doubts about her ability to duplicate her winning performance. We would not risk a dime on this filly under these circumstances.

As it turned out, even the public wasn't fooled by Miss Houston's glamorous last race, for she was made fifth in the betting at post time. It was not surprising that she made the pace for a half-mile. Nor was it surprising that she had nothing left thereafter, and was beaten twelve lengths by Debate, with Finkie second and Grand Opera third.

The third race is a four and a half furlong sprint for two-year-old maiden colts and geldings, all but one being first-time starters.

The fourth is a six-furlong claimer for 3-year-old fillies. There are only two hides in this scramble with positive 1/p's: Pomp's Favorite and Cross Up. Of these, Pomp's Favorite is still a maiden with a way far-out 1/p. Neither of these two has raced since March 13.

It is not my wish to lead the student-fan into bad habits, but this race is interesting to me and I would have fudged a little on the control system, simply because Gross Up is the only possible play here and she's going postward at a handsome overlay under the circumstances.

Let's look at her and see why. She won her race on February 16 at Bowie under a drive, so could not be expected to win her next. She was beaten eight lengths in her race on March 2, then ran an improved race on March 13, closing from pre-stretch to finish to be beaten by four and a half lengths, an improvement of three and three-quarters lengths over her previous one. It would appear she is tightening up again after the February win. Then, on March 29, she worked three furlongs on a fast track in 36 feconds flat. This is standard, and a further indication that she has recovered her edge after the hard-win.

Yes, I know we are not using workouts with this control where the 15-day time limit has been passed, but in this case it *is* additional testimony that Cross Up did not lose too much by her month-old win, and is now definitely about to come to hand. Then, when the betting public overlooked her and let her go postward at 8 to 1, it was just too big a temptation for me—and she did have two Md Sp Wt contests in her past performances.

Since we have every reason to expect we're not going to find many qualified plays because of disqualifications on time limit, I would feel justified in fudging. So, while I would have qualified Cross Up for my own personal action, I would not expect the student-fan to digress in order to catch this good one.

I see I have neglected to mention Smileabit as a contender

in this race. She was off her race at Bowie on March 26 and she won this one by two lengths, which might give us the impression that she would have something left. But her trainer knew better. In a desperate try for another purse, and to get a small advantage of two pounds impost, he took Jockey Barnes off— the boy who had ridden her so capably in her winning effort —and substituted a double-bug(**) apprentice. He might just as well have hung a sign on Smileabit that she had nothing left.

The fifth race at Laurel was a mile and one-eight claimer for fillies and mares. You might as well get used to it, fellers and gals. Laurel is one of those tracks that attracts a lot of female horses to their barnes—one of the reasons I don't rate it as one of my favorite tracks.

There's no problem in this race, since none of the contestants can be qualified as contenders. All, without an exception, have nothing but claimers in their past performances.

The sixth gives more promise. It's a six-furlong claimer for 4-year-olds and upward, and of the twelve starters only two are fillies. This is more like it from the contestant's viewpoint, but we are still up against the time limit disadvantage. This is always trying at the early spring meetings as well as at the early winter meetings. It usually takes several weeks, for instance, before we can begin to get an accurate condition line on the horses brought in from all over the country for the first winter meeting of the Florida season—Tropical Park. Though Sunshine Park comes somewhat later, it does not attract the same class of contender, so here, too, the condition problem is an acute one until the meeting has progressed about two weeks. In these early weeks, to get any action at all, I have to resort entirely to an analysis of workouts. This can be risky business and I am not going to ask the student-fan to indulge in it, for it is still far better for the tyro to limit his play rather than cut his plus percentages too thin.

Six of the contestants are disposed of out of hand on time limit. Of the remainder, Allahgem, Crooked Question, and Eden Hall will have to be dropped for lack of present condition. This leaves Bob Robby, Hampo, and Doctor Bern as contenders.

Bob Robby turned in a creditable effort at Bowie on March 20 after a five-month layoff, only to fade from third by a neck to fifth by two lengths in the run to the wire. Hampo backed up six lengths in the stretch-drive in his last, March 24 at Bowie. Both he and Bob Robby have positive 1/p's.

Doctor Bern ran a closing race all the way from first call to finish in his last, at Bowie on March 20, to be beaten by a nose in a photo finish. He appearently tried hard for a win and may have used himself up, since this was a much faster race than either of his two wins at Narragansett Park last December and November. It was a sterling effort after being long rested, but would be a risky speculation. The best we can say for Bob Robby and Hampo is that both show some improvement, but probably not enough to expect either to be able to turn in a winning effort today. So we're going to call this a tie, and not a very exciting one, and pass the race.

In the seventh race, only Ji-Jo could be qualfiied on time limit. He has eight A1w in his record, but backed up all the way in his last race to set up a negative 1/p.

Whoops! I missed Iris H. This mare raced on March 24 at Bowie, but may not have completely recovered her form after a hard-fought win on March 8. Also, she has a negative 1/p. We have to rate this as a doubtful race, and pass.

The eighth is an allowance affair and the feature race of the day. It's for 4-year-olds and upward, to be contested at six furlongs.

Three of the starters have stakes races in their class lines. These are Creswood Dottie, Tuscan Spy, and Trojan Jewel. None of them has raced recently enough to be of interest to us, so we pass this one also.

I might interject a word of advice at this point. If a student-fan plans to play an "early meeting" such as this one, work it and keep a record from opening day, by all means, but do not participate until most of the stables have sent their horses out at least once. Those first two weeks could be most discouraging for the novice, and costly. After about two weeks, you will begin to see that you can start to qualify enough of them on the condition factor, so that you will be able to make selections with a reasonable degree of confidence. This is time enough to think about unlimbering the bankroll.

The nightcap at Laurel on April 2 was a claimer on the turf course for 4-year-olds and upward, to be contested at one mile and a sixteenth. Possible contenders are Sunaqua, Bay Hornet, Image, and English Sole.

Sunaqua won his last going away by two lengths. He also won his previous race (March 19) going away. Neither of these wins seems to have taken too much out of him, although he did not win his last by as wide a margin as the previous one, and thus has a slightly negative 1/p. This could be taken with a grain of salt if we were strainiing for action—which, of course, we are. Now, when we're *straining* to try to qualify something, we are vulnerable, so we must be especially on guard at a time like this. But since both of Sunaqua's recent races were strong closers from first call to finish, we would probably be justified in at least holding him in abeyance until we look at the others.

Bay Hornet faded a bit in his last in the run to the wire, but he has a borderline 1/p with less than a length improvement. Image backed up badly all the way in his last and displays a strongly negative 1/p. We drop them both from further consideration.

English Sole was out last in an allowance on March 28 at Bowie. His last race, though not too bad, was nothing to go into ecstasies over, either. At the first call he was second, five lengths off the pace; at the pre-stretch call, he was second, six lengths back; at the in-stretch call, he was still second and still six lengths back. He wound up third, beaten by five and three-quarters lengths. But in his race on March 19 at Bowie he was beaten by twelve lengths, so he has a positive 1/p—which we would like much better if his last-race pattern hadn't been so lackadaisical. From this we find it hard to believe that English Sole has edge enough yet for a winning effort. We would much prefer to go along with Sunaqua, who has recently demonstrated, twice, that he *does* have his winning edge.

Perhaps if playable selections were not so hard to come by, at Laurel, and at this early point in the brand-new spring meeting, we could afford to let this one run for Sweeney. But we have only one selection so far, and we had to fudge to get that one. It boils down, then, to the question of going along with a horse with two strongly closing races in a row, but with a slightly negative 1/p (even though both races were won going away), as compared with a horse with a positive 1/p, but whose last two races were decidedly indifferent. I am strongly tempted to take Sunaqua as another fudged qualifier, and with the understanding that I do *not* recommend this practice for the student-fan until he has acquired the necessary experience to know when to fudge and when not to.

Actually, then, there would have been no qualifiers all day if we had stuck relentlessly to our class-condition requirements.

The two horses we fudged to qualify both won. Cross Up paid $18.00, $11.60, and $6.20. Sunaqua paid $7.80, $5.40, and $3.60.

Let's move on to Aqueduct, where the meeting has been under way since March 20; hence, we shall not be so hand-cuffed by lack of recent racing.

The first race at Aqueduct is a one-mile cakewalk for 3-year-old maidens.

Lone Voyager has four AlwM and two Md Sp Wt in his past performances, and he's been risked only once in a claimer, for an $8,000 tag. Today's claiming price is $3,500. He closed a strong seven lengths in his last, but it was on March 8 (at Santa Anita) so we have to disqualify him, though he has worked twice at the Belmont training track since being shipped here from the West Coast.

Pryoly has raced twice here since shipping up from Florida, the first on opening day (March 20) and the last on March 27. He qualifies on time limit. And he has one Md Sp Wt in his past performances so he can be considered a contender. Neither of these races was strong enough to indicate to us that this hide has any winning potential at the present time, though his 1/p is mildly positive; but that tells us only that he improved a bit over his previous race and is therefore in a little better shape than he was on opening day. We'll hold him in abeyance, but with a mental reservation.

Heliopoli can be qualified on time limit, having had an outing in a cheap claimer on March 23 here at Aqueduct. And he has two A1wM (Md Allow) and two Md Sp Wt to qualify him as a contender on class by association. So far, so good. That last race of his was a sharp one. He was running third by a neck at the first call; second by a head at the pre-stretch call; took command by a half-length entering the stretch, but was short in the run to the wire, finishing second, beaten by a length. But his previous race (at New Orleans before shipping north) tells us that he shipped well and has been working well, for he was beaten off by twelve lengths at the Fair Grounds, so he now displays a positive 1/p. He's a qualifier so far.

Great Run has had two outings here at Aqueduct since shipping north from Hialeah. In both, he backed up badly, though the last was somewhat better than the previous race, giving him a positive 1/p. We'll look back on him later. For now, he's a contender by virtue of recent racing and four Md Sp Wt efforts in his performance line.

Atlantic Avenue is another that has shipped here from Santa Anita and has already had one outing here, on March 27. This was a good race. While not a perfect pattern, it was a definite indicator of good present form. Sixth by eight and a half lengths at the first call, he moved up to fifth by three and three-quarter lengths at the pre-stretch call; then got shuffled a bit coming around the bend to be fourth, four and a half lengths back, at the in-stretch call; then came on to close two and a half lengths in the run for the money. He finished third, beaten by only two lengths. This was a considerable improvement over his previous finish at Santa Anita, so he also displays a positive 1/p.

Swell the Sail cannot be qualified as a contender for he shows nothing but maiden claimers in his performance line.

Jim C. has an Alw at Tropical and a Md Sp Wt at Hialeah prior to shipping north, where he had an outing here at Aqueduct on March 22. His 1/p is positive, being one of those way-way-out fringe things—17/44.

Bascom's Folly, Elliott's Charm, and Spoon Shot are not contenders, since they have only claiming races in their performance lines.

Of our first round of contender qualifiers, we can now retire Pryoly, Great Run, and Jim C., since their last-race patterns do not compare favorably with those of Heliopoli and Atlantic Avenue. Okay?

Since we have reason to believe we are not going to be hamstrung on recent condition, as we were at Laurel, we feel no urge to attempt to separate our two remaining, tied contenders. Besides this, there are no less than six horses in this race from whom we have reason to expect improved racing. Seven, really. I refer to Lone Voyager and Spoon Shot, besides our first-round contenders, all of whom also had positive 1/p. With this much condition contention the race is a risky one, since there is really no one horse that stands out over his competition. And, we will recall, we already have a winner in Miney Myerson, a speed-conversion selection in the second race.

We'll pass this first race. No need to strain.

We move on to the third, since there is no need to gild the Miney Myerson lily.

The third at Aqueduct is a five-furlong dash for 2-year-old maiden fillies. Too many of these have had only one race, or no race at all, for us to make an intelligent comparison.

The fourth at Aqueduct is a starter handicap for 3-year-olds and upward, a little early in the year to be asking three-year-olds to compete against older horses. Only one accepted: Mr. General, a 3-year-old colt.

While Mr. General is given a very generous advantage in the weights (108 pounds as against 122 for Irish Dandy, for instance), it is a losing proposition to play these younger horses in older company, and we make it a rule never to do so—not until fall, when the youngsters have attained growth, strength, and experience.

I do not mean by this that a 3-year-old *never* beats older horses in the early months of the year, only that it's a decidedly unprofitable risk.

A so-called starter handicap is not a good type of race to begin with, as witness the condition in this one: ". . . which have started for a claiming price of $5,000, or less, since October 3, 1961." How ambiguous can you get?

So, we do not like this race to begin with, and we're well satisfied when it culminates in a tie between Charlie Z. and Prepal, which we do not consider it worth the effort to attempt to separate.

The next race, the fifth on the April 2 card at Aqueduct, is a good old, honest $5,000 claimer for four-year-olds and upward. This is to be contested at seven furlongs, with eight starters left after scratches.

Challenge Baby, with a race at Aqueduct on March 26 and a promising last-race pattern, is the only one in the race with positive 1/p. But we cannot qualify him, because he has nothing but claimers in his class line.

The sixth is a $10,000 claimer for 3-year-olds, going six furlongs. At a glance, we see that Shiny Button has the outstandingly best class line. Besides five allowance races, this three-year-old gelding raced in The City of Miami Beach at Tropical, and in the Dade Met H, also at Tropical. (These would be called out as A1wS and HcpS in the *Form*.) None of the other contestants has a class line that would closely compare with this, so our effort will be to qualify Shiny Button. If we cannot, there will be time enough to move on to the others.

Shiny Button's last race was at one mile (at Aqueduct on March 22), which qualifies him as a contender. His last-race pattern was good, considering it was his first start here after shipping north from Hialeah. He was second, two lengths off the pace at the first call; was forcing the pace by a half-length at the pre-stretch call; and was breathing in Our Breed's ear, only a neck back, at the in-stretch; but he was short in the run to the wire. A strong race, even though it wasn't a perfect pattern. We feel safe in assuming that he will improve off this race. As an added fillip, his 1/p is strongly positive.

Shiny Button qualifies all the way. Though our mind is all but made up, it would be folly not to look at the rest so as to determine what Shiny Button is up against.

Cinder Man, with one A1w to his credit and a race here at Aqueduct on March 24, could ordinarily be rated as a contender. However, his last race, after shipping here from Gulfstream Park, leaves something to be desired. Perhaps he did not ship well. In any case, he shows a steady fade from first call to finish, which tends to dim his positive 1/p.

Banker Bob, with a positive 1/p, also shows a steady fade from first call to finish and has only one Md Sp Wt for class by association.

Nest Egg, another recent competitor, with two races here at Aqueduct since shipping north from Hialeah, has but two Md Sp Wt outings in his class line. Hardly comparable to Shiny Button's glittery class line. However, Nest Egg did run a strong race in that last on March 29. He lost a length in the run from first call to pre-stretch, then settled in stride and took command by three at the in-stretch call, drawing away by six lengths at the finish. A good race. An easy win. If he showed more class by association, he would worry us a bit.

Prize Fight has one Alw in his class line, and a race on March 21. He has a positive 1/p, but he lost ground steadily from the pre-stretch call to the finish. Not quite ready.

Lorne Fox closed well from in-stretch to finish in his race on March 24, but has nothing but claimers in his past performance line, so we pass him by, after a glance at his negative 1/p.

Lightness we pass into the discard for the same reasons. Scarteen, with one Alw at Pimlico and a race here on March 24, could be classed as a contender. But he lost ground steadily from the pre-stretch call to finish and has a negative 1/p.

Nest Egg appears to be the one to beat on the recent condition factor, but he doesn't have the kind of class by associtaion that is so noticeable in Shiny Button's performance line.

Our initial judgment is sustained. Shiny Button is the play.

The seventh race is the feature at Aqueduct. It is the twenty-third running of The Correction, an HcpS for fillies and mares, 3-year-olds and upward. No three-year-old picked up the challenge in this one. They are all four and older—ten of them (Seven Thirty was scratched) going six furlongs for $20,000 added.

You will remember that we leave class and condition pretty much up to the trainer in a race of this quality. Our assumption is that each and every contestant is ready to go all out for this kind of money. There is only one filly in there we'd be inclined to disqualify out of hand. She is Dream On, and this will be her first outing in stakes company. The rest all show at least one HcpS in their performance lines. We look at the box scores for a win-ability line, and find that both Staretta and Bright Holly have won nine of their starts. Rose O'Neill has eight and Smashing Gail seven.

If we strained, we might be able to affect a separation here, but we do not wish to strain, not for a filly and mare stake, bless 'em. We are content to watch this one and wait to see if we can uncover a more sound speculation in the final two stanzas of the day.

Smashing Gail took the pace away from Staretta after leaving the half-mile pole, and won by two and a half lengths with something left. Rose O'Neill was second. And Bright Holly.

The eighth was a $15,000 claimer for 4-year-olds and upward, going one mile.

Barracho J. J. raced strongly in his first outing at Aqueduct after shipping in from Santa Anita. We must assume that he shipped well. He had an outing in the San Francisco Handicap (stake) at Tranforan, and also had an A1w there. He qualifies as a contender. His last race, while a stout one, was not a perfect closing pattern, but he was never more than a head out of it all the way. While this may be read as a hard race, he has had a fourteen-day rest, and that should be enough for a horse with a touch of stakes class—the only one in the race, incidentally, that has been out in a stakes event. Remember this. It may be the edge that could decide the race. And his strongly positive 1/p appeals to us.

Ruffy, with a long line of A1w races and two claimers, raced last on March 28. He is a contender at this point. His last race, at one and one-eighth miles, was a good one. He was in contention all the way to finish second, beaten by only three-quarters of a length. And his 1/p is positive.

Rulamyth is far off form. He was beaten by eighteen lengths in his last, and by twelve lengths in his previous, for a negative 1/p. We drop him.

Flang Dang has seven Alw in his performance line and a recent mile race that he won going away by two lengths. This was a closing effort all the way. Flang Dang won this under a mild drive, probably not enough pressure to appreciably hurt his chances today. His 1/p is positive.

Count Eric showed a little urge to run for a half-mile, then hung. His 1/p ($\frac{7}{8}$), though mildly positive, does not stand comparison with the others. Sir Barker lost ground all the way after an alert start and has a negative 1/p. Not for us. Rudolph we disqualify on time limit, since his last race was on March 9.

We have three sound contenders in this one: Barracho J. J., Ruffy, and Flang Dang.

This is not an easy separation. Flang Dang is the high weight with 122 pounds, but he carried 121 successfully in his last. Still, he is yielding six pounds to Barracho J. J. and four to Ruffy. And strictly from a speed standpoint, his standard conversion rating was the slowest of the three, a minus two (-2).

There is a jockey switch, from Baeza to Ycaza, on Barracho J. J., but we do not consider this particularly significant. It's a question of Baeza's being Flang Dang's regular jockey and riding him today, whereas Barracho J. J.'s trainer had to seek elsewhere for riding talent, and was fortunate in getting Ycaza, a very capable saddlesmith. Rotz is again in the irons aboard Ruffy.

No, we have not lost sight of Barracho J. J.'s touch of stakes class, and the difference should be enough. Also, Barracho J. J.'s minus fourteen (-14) would seem to testify to his superior class, though Ruffy's minus 8 (-8) was creditable.

Perhaps such a tight race as this is a challenge. In any case, we are reluctant to pass it, though we would not take any student-fan to task who put it in the doubtful category. But because of his touch of stakes class, amply verified by his -14 standard speed rating, we personally are willing to nominate Barracho J. J.

Then, when we finally check the odds, question our wisdom,

for Barracho J. J. is going postward at even money. While we still consider him the most likely winner, he appears to be an underlay as an even-money favorite.

But we have already stuck our neck out and this certainly should be an interesting race to watch, so let's see what happens.

This race, at one mile, breaks out of the chute way over yonder, for Aqueduct is a 1⅛-mile oval. I mention this because the mile tracks, which most major ovals are, start the mile run directly in front of the grandstand.

They're all in the gate. The flag goes up, and the buzz of the crowd dies away to a tense hush.

The bell jangles. The gates slam open—and they're off and running.

At the start, it's Barracho J. J. Ruffy is second. And Rulamyth.

Around the far turn—it's Rulamyth by a half-length. Barracho J. J. is second, one length ahead of Flang Dang. Ruffy is now fourth. On the top of the turn, Rulamyth is still setting the pace by a half-length. Barracho J. J. is forcing the issue from second place. Count Eric is third, one length before Ruffy, who has come on again. Flang Dang is fifth.

Into the stretch turn—Rulamyth increases his advantage to one full length. Barracho J. J. is still content to hold second place. Ruffy is third.

Around the turn and into the stretch. Jockey Ycaza asks Barracho J. J. the question. His response is a two-length lead as they straighten out for the run to the wire. Rulamyth is second, one length before Ruffy. Count Eric is fourth and Flang Dang fifth.

Barracho J. J., displaying his class, opens another two lengths, to win going away by four. Ruffy is second. And Flang

Dang puts on a belated challenge to get up for third. Which is exactly the way our speed separation placed them.

Barracho's easy-win was made in somewhat slower time than his best. If he is not pitched too high in his next, he should be good for another win.

Now let's take a look at the nightcap. This is a $5,000 claimer for 4-year-olds and upward, going seven furlongs.

Fire Trail, Route Sixty-Six, Moon Again, Nilo's Son, Artica, and Pawanson all have to be discarded on time limit. This leaves us Electioneer, Ufo, and Solar Flare.

All three of these have positive 1/p's and alert last races within the time limit, with Ufo showing somewhat the best pattern. But neither he nor Electioneer can be qualified as contenders, since neither has anything but claiming races in his past performance line. Class by association, then, hands the race to Solar Flare on a silver platter by virtue of his five Alw races at Hazel Park and Detroit, his strong last race—in which he was short in the run to the wire, but should improve today —and his positive 1/p.

I rarely wait for the last race. Invariably, I have my daily stipend long before then, and leave the nightcap for those desperate people who are frantically trying to get out of the barrel. After-the-races traffic is a headache I try to avoid, so if I have a satisfactory profit by the time the feature race comes up, I leave.

Which is neither here nor there insofar as this nightcap is concerned, for Solar Flare does qualify on our class-condition control, and we are trying to give the student-fan a complete picture of possible action—and reaction. For Solar Flare does substantiate our previous reminder that *nobody* wins them all. This ninth stanza has won by Ufo, with Solar Flare winding up in the show spot.

Here is our day's work sheet, including Miney Myerson, who had been previously qualified on speed-conversion.

RACE	HORSE	WIN	PLACE	SHOW
2	Miney Myerson	$9.00	$4.80	$3.40
6	Shiny Button	14.30	6.60	4.00
8	Barracho J. J.	4.10	2.70	2.20
9	Solar Flare	...	...	2.80

A good day, in spite of Sollar Flare—and nobody forced us to play the nightcap did they?

CHAPTER TWELVE *Rounding out the Complex*

We have now checked six different tracks, covering a wide variety of locales, competition, and the two most difficult seasons for most fans. We have combined our speed-conversion control with class-condition control—which in itself is a complex of controls—into a powerful, mechanical selection procedure that should not be beyond the ken of any student-fan who is willing to bring the time and study to a million-dollar goal.

What we have combined so far should really provide enough action for anyone. But I know my horseplayers. It is only the dyed-in-the-wool pro who is content to wait for his spots. It bothers him not at all when a beastie that he's passed up as a risky speculation wins, with him holding no tickets. For he knows that by being choosy he also avoids many losers, and he wants the biggest yield possible from his investments.

So does the inexperienced fan, but too often he has the mistaken idea that he must play every race so as not to miss out on anything. If he has done his work well and is a good selector, he may still make a profit, but he will never make the maximum by manufacturing a play where none exists.

Percentage of yield increases in direct proportion to the amount of critical care that is brought to the chore of qualifying a selection—or of disqualifying a borderline, or risky, speculation.

There is a way, however, to get more action—and we mean relatively safe and profitable action—though at the cost of sacrificing percentage of yield.

This is by a modified "dutching" in those races where several horses figure too close together to separate by any means other than a crystal ball. "Dutching," then, should be resorted to in only those races that we have already carefully figured, and for reason have relegated to the doubtful list, but which we feel we have reduced to a group within which the eventual winner lies.

"Dutching," it should be explained at this point, was used successfully by certain smarties back in the old bookmaking days before the advent of the pari-mutuels.

It was possible then, if you were fleet enough of foot and sharp enough of mind, to shop around among the bookmaker stalls for variations in odds and, in some cases, to lay a bet on every horse in the race and still be sure of a profit, no matter which one won. The reason for this was that the old-time bookmaker made his book on the basis of 120 per cent. Thus, after all bets were paid, he could expect to have that 20 per cent still in hand for his work of handling the action.

Under the pari-mutuel system, it is no longer possible to "dutch" every horse in a given race and come up with a consistent profit. Naturally, even under pari-mutuel, there *are* times when a lopsided long shot wins and it would be profitable to have bought a corner on each horse going. But these occasions are not frequent enough to yield an over-all profit. So, when we refer to "dutching" now, we refer to a modified form of it, in which we have already reduced the probables to a controllable group but have not been able to pinpoint any certain one.

Because it is necessary to do all the work first, it can readily be seen why the "dutching" aspect of our control complex has been left more or less sketchy until now. For we will apply it only to those races that have proven otherwise unplayable.

For this, and because we can now afford to relax our controls a bit, we will use 1/p as our basic factor and, where necessary, we will extend our 15-day limit to thirty days. Conversely, where there are too many qualifiers—we will make three our top limit—we can tighten up on the time limit to exclude the least likely contenders.

As an example, and because it should still be fresh in our mind, let's re-examine that nightcap at Aqueduct, assuming that we had been unable to qualify Solar Flare as a contender, or for some other reason had to disqualify him.

We would then have been faced with a group of three horses with positive 1/p, strictly a condition group without regard to the class-by-association feature.

In this case, all three would be playable on a flat-bet basis, since Ufo, the shortest price of the three, was quoted at 3 to 1 on the approximate odds board, and the other two, Electioneer and Solar Flare, at 7 to 2. Thus, if any one of these three converts, there will be a profit.

As we already know, Ufo won the race. He paid $8.80. Since we had six dollars invested (figured on a $2 minimum basis for simplicity) the profit would have been $2.80. Apart from the small profit, and we do occasionally take less playing only one (Barracho J. J., for instance), the extra action is an emotional salve that some players *must* have. It could be said, then, that our modified dutching control is the tranquilizer of the complex.

It might be argued that virtually the same small profit might be made, in the doubtful races, by playing only one of them to show, and there is something to be said for this. But for one thing, some fans have a conditioned reflex against playing other than to win. The most important reason for playing three to win, however, is that a race that is on the doubtful list to begin with could easily result in the one we selected for show action being run all the way out of the money, due to a traffic problem or some other reason, while it is less likely that all three of our selections would encounter trouble.

Here's another thing to consider: Most races we will use in this manner will offer a better odds spread than the example we have used, and a nice fat long shot could well be the one to convert, giving us a much larger profit margin.

Some of the races we have passed by will still remain unplayable. For instance, in that first race at Aqueduct there were no less than seven horses that would have come into the picture on positive 1/p. Even after eliminating two of them (as outside the 15-day limit), we would still have five, and we have set our limit at three. The third race, also at Aqueduct, did not furnish us with enough line to figure on 1/p of any kind for most of the starters. But there will be others that will come into line for play as dutching vehicles and which will enhance both our action and our profits.

There is one thing we must keep in mind, however. With our dutching prodecure, we *are* dealing with races that in our first judgment were classified as doubtful. Even by letting down the bars on requirements to make two or three horses playable, we have no assurance that we will now tab the winner in every case. Actually, what we are counting on in this prodecure is the occasional fat long shot that we will catch.

For instance, in that fourth race at Laurel Park, where we strained a bit to get Cross Up in line (and we did say we would blame no conservative fan for passing this), we could now qualify both Cross Up and Pomp's Favorite under the dutching control and catch the $18 payoff that the conservative among us would otherwise have missed.

Or in the third race at Laurel, where we did not choose to make a separation, we could now qualify both Miss Houston and Debate on positive 1/p, and thereby catch the $8.40 payoff returned by Debate.

In each of these races we had only two with positive 1/p. We made no attempt to bring in anything else simply because there was room for one more on our three-horse limit.

The fifth, still at Laurel, a race which we had to pass before because none had other than claimers in their past performances, we now can bring in under the dutching control, for two of these had positive 1/p: San Sebastian and Entourage.

San Sebastian won this race and returned $20.80, $7.00, and $3.60 across the board. Entourage showed.

In the sixth at Laurel, Bob Robby and Hampo would now come into line for play—and we had a losing race here. Cromwellian, the winner, a hide with two strong races, the last within our extended 30-day limit, had a negative 1/p after a win.

In the seventh race, we find a different kind of problem, which may not occur often but which we should know how to handle when it does crop up. There is only one hide in this race who has a positive 1/p and a last race even within the extended 30-day limit: Part Time Indian. And since only one horse qualifying robs us of the added fillip of several who might convert for us and thus no longer constitutes a dutching plan, and since we did not see fit to take a chance on this one in the original control, we would still have to pass the race. Okay? Part Time Indian did run second, however.

There is a third limitation that it seems wise to invoke. We will *not resort to dutching in the feature race* of the day.

So, even Laurel, where we had a difficult time qualifying any action, now is brought into the fold, safely and profitably, by the use of our modified dutching control.

It will be noted also that, while we have let the bars down considerably, we have compensated for this risk by playing more than one contestant. Thus, we still have *control* over our operation.

Where before we had only two plays at Laurel, both of them fudged a bit and so inaccessible to the conservative fan, we now have a good spread of action, and a substantial profit for the day. Through dutching, we have brought this otherwise desolate day into perspective.

We would have gained nothing on this day at Gulfstream Park through dutching, but there we already had a good spread of action, and profit, without dutching.

Going backward, now, to our three winter tracks, let's see if our "tranquilizer" control helps any.

In the fifth at the Fair Grounds in New Orleans, we had no qualified play before and we have none now, for there are far too many qualified with positive 1/p. A race with so much visual present condition is definitely up for grabs. In such a race, it is virtually impossible to predetermine which hide will improve the most, and therefore walk off with the winner's end of the purse.

In the sixth race at Fair Grounds, we could qualify both Hawaiian Music and Sun Ponder for dutching action. And they finished one, two. Sun Ponder paid $5.20, $3.40, and $2.80. Hawaiian Music paid $4.00 and $3.00 for place and show. Had there been three qualifiers, which is our set limit for dutching, we would have been stopped on the short odds. To play three, our minimum break-even odds on the heavier backed contestant would naturally be 2 to 1, or an anticipated $6-plus payoff on this shortest one. There is little point in dutching unless we can see a good possibility of a profit.

So, when we have a dutching spread lined up, it makes good sense to consult the Tote Board a few minutes before "off" time to see if the odds will at least take care of our investment in case the shortest priced one should win.

Now let's look in on Hialeah again. In the first race (which we had to pass in both first and second control scrutinies), it now appears possible that we may be able to uncover a dutching play. Yes, there are three horses with positive 1/p: Fausta, Galan, and On the Quiet. Galan was made the lukewarm favorite in this stanze at 3 to 1, which would anticipate a payoff of $8-plus should he win. Since there are three qualifiers, our investment would be six dollars. Okay.

On the Quiet won this waltz and paid $24.60, $10.20, and $6.70 across the board.

In the sixth race, we again encounter entirely too much visual condition to hold out any hope of ever being able to snag a winner with a dutching spread. There are no less than nine qualifiers on 1/p and recentness. It is truly a wide-open affair—an excellent chance for a long shot to grab it all, if we could pinpoint him. But there is nothing we can do but watch a tussle like this. Big Art, one of the nine qualifiers, took them all into camp with a wire-to-wire effort, and returned $49.80, $17.90, and $12.00.

In the eighth, we find we can qualify Linger On, Iron Core, and Thunder Hill on positive 1/p and recentness.

The shortest price on these three is 2 to 1 for Linger On. Thunder Hill is 5 to 1 and Iron Core 11 to 1. If Linger On should convert, we could expect small change for a profit. If either of the others should win, we would have a substantial profit. The race is okay for play.

Linger On *did* win this, but in a hard, neck decision over Winterish who was coupled in an entry with Thunder Hill. So we missed a $12 payoff by a couple of whiskers, and got $6.30 instead for Linger On's win.

So, by dutching we picked up one nice long shot and one skin-of-the-teeth thirty cents—but still on the profit side.

Bespoken, in the nightcap, we had already tagged.

At Santa Anita, in the first race, we will recall that we qualified City Babe via class-condition, so we now reexamine the second race for a possible dutching play.

Six horses—Miller's Pride, Pirate Cove, Johnson's Choice, Valdura, Kowaliga, and Pampas Legend—all have raced recently enough and have positive 1/p. This is too many. We have set a limit of three for dutching.

We would have to be desperate indeed to attempt a further separation in a 3-year-old maiden race, and we are not desperate. We have already selected a qualified play in the first race and several others. We are not starved. Common sense tells us that almost anything could happen here, and probably will. By now, we have worked enough with this complex control system to know that we will get plenty of action, and plenty of profits, to send us along toward our million-dollar goal without running unnecessary risks.

In case you're curious, Pirate Cove won the race.

In the sixth race, if you remember, we reduced the playable field to three. Then I went off on a tangent to show how I personally would have further reduced these to one playable. But since this play was purely my own unorthodox finagling, it was not listed for the record. So this still rates as a passed race. But, accepting the three—Gun Box, Daiichi, and Sweet Lilly— we now have the maximum spread for a dutching play. So we check the approximate odds on the Tote Board. Daiichi is the favorite in the betting at 2 to 1. Gun Box is second choice at 7 to 2. Sweet Lilly is third choice at 5 to 1.

This can be played. Should Daiichi win, we will get our

investment back, plus some odd change. If either of the others convert, our profit will be a little more substantial.

Let's watch them run.

At the start, it's Daiichi taking the lead. Inoorpapa is second. And Dimity.

At the quarter, it's Gun Box on top by a head. Inoorpapa is second a half-length before Daiichi. Sweet Lilly was slow to start and is now tenth, way back yonder.

Coming to the half-mile pole, it's Gun Box by one and a half lengths. Inoorpapa is second by two lengths. Long Ears is now third and Garden Fresh fourth. Daiichi is through early and dropping back steadily.

Around the turn and into the stretch, it's Gun Box by four lengths. Long Ears is second—and Inoorpapa. Daiichi is now ninth and Sweet Lilly still tenth.

Shoemaker lets Gun Box coast down to the wire, winning by two and three-quarter lengths. Long Ears is second. And Garden Fresh gets through for third.

Gun Box paid $9.20, $6.40, and $5.60.

And so to the nightcap at Santa Anita. We had to pass this one before insofar as class-condition control was concerned. Maybe there's a dutching possibility here, though, frankly, we should be on our way home by now. However, I *do* usually work the whole card, if I have time, before going to the track, and a little extra investigation doesn't harm anybody.

But no! There are five nags qualified as to both recentness (15 days) and positive 1/p. Here, we could undoubtedly figure some way to eliminate two of these, if we were desperate to get out of the barrel, which we are not. So we pass it to those who are.

By now, the student-fan should have a pretty solid understanding of how to proceed with his own personal workout.

Form here on, it's up to you. I could go on and on, working example after example for you and it would not add any more to your know how. From this point, you learn by doing, with as much reference back to the text as you need as you go along. As the workout progresses toward a minimum thousand-race trial run, your facility at handling the whole complex will increase. You will make fewer and fewer mistakes. Your percentage of winning races will go up and up. Your confidence in yourself, and in the control complex, will soar.

You will find yourself checking for every part of the control complex as you work each race, instead of going through the *Form* or *Telegraph* three times, as we have done for clarity.

You will begin to see things clearly in the past performances that you never before dreamed were there. Some of these things will give you the *GO* sign, some the *STOP*. Some will be warning lights only, which if not heeded or carefully balanced will result in your backing losers later. And the fewer losers we back, the sooner we arrive at the million-dollar mark.

So take enough time to do a thorough job of selecting, and when you do select a loser—and I'm referring to your on-paper check—go back to that race and rework it to see if you overlooked something. Thus, it may be that you can learn from your mistakes—if you did make a boo-boo. If it still figures the same way for you, you will at least know you did your work well, and you can take what solace there is in your knowledge that nobody wins them all. And while you're at it, you might read the chart caller's comments at the bottom of the results charts. From this, you may learn what happened to your well-chosen selection—for there *is* a reason for everything that happens in racing.

CHAPTER THIRTEEN

Proving the Pudding

We are now ready to see what kind of actual cash our brainchild is capable of producing. You have seen that our control complex has picked a goodly number of winners, and in some cases at rather handsome payoffs. But you are probably wondering how even that adds up to a million dollars. And *if* it does, now long will it take and how much investment is involved? And how will the money action be controlled? Can we run a two-dollar bill into a million? Or is this going to take a well-financed corporation to swing it?

Good questions. Important questions. And we have no intention of bringing you this far just to leave you hanging on a cloud.

As we have said before, the greatest percentage of yield is to be earned from flat wagering. In other words, keeping the unit of investment the same at all times, even when we are sure our selection is a mortal cinch and the temptation is strong to go overboard.

So what unit should we use?

That will have to be governed, or controlled, by the amount of investment capital each of you individually has available. Thus, because of the high percentage of winners you should get—and I *do* mean after you have completed your minimum thousand-race workout—your flat investment should never be more than 10 per cent of your investment bankroll, and at most tracks, where the mutuel "handle" is not astronomical, $200 flat is about as high as it would be sensible to go, for a heavier investment would almost certainly hurt your odds appreciably.

More specifically, if you have only $20 available, your betting must remain at $2.00 flat, until you have increased the bankroll to a point where you can safely move on up to $4 or $5—and so on up until you have an investment bankroll of $2,000, at which time you can wager the suggested $200 maximum.

When you *must* start with a small unit and build the capital up over a period of time, the unit remains the same after a loss as it was when you backed the loser. In other words, if you invested $25 and lost, your next selection should be backed with another $25 investment. You do not regress after a loss. Neither do you progress to try to make up the loss. You remain on the same level until your capital has increased to the point where 10 per cent of the total calls for a larger investment.

It should also be obvious that the $200 limit is a generalization. At some tracks, where the "handle" is comparatively small, even this much might reduce your return. At others, catering to large population centers, many races will be so heavily played that a $2,000 investment would not appreciably alter the odds.

Obviously, then, if you are in a hurry to get up into the millionaire class, you should head for the big operations. I have seen mutuel pools so large—at Santa Anita, for instance —that a $5,000 wager would alter the odds only about fifty cents.

So you see, I cannot answer your question as to how long it should take to make a million. It depends too much on the individual, how much starting capital he will have available, and where he plans to operate.

The best way to demonstrate what *can* be done, we think, is to use the $200 flat wager and run off a few work sheets, then add up the scores, strike an average, and draw your conclusions from that.

Let's look first at the week's selections we made at the Fair Grounds in New Orleans. This is a good average track. It hardly reaches the proportions of a big operation like Aqueduct, but it's far larger than Charles Town or Sunshine Park. Here, $200 flat play should certainly not be excessive.

Here's our work sheet. This is for the first week—six racing days—in February, 1962.

DATE	RACE	HORSE	WIN MUTUEL	WAGER	GROSS RETURN
2/1	1	Gold Robin	$ 6.80	$200	$ 680
	2	Pat's Folly	32.40	"	3,240
	6	In the Barrel ⎱ *dutch* Sun Ponder ⎰	. . . 5.20	" "	—— 520
	8	Orleans Doge	2.80	"	280
	9	Quiboy	6.80	"	680
				$1,200	$5,400 1,200
				NET GAIN	$4,200
2/2	4	Manuscript ⎱ Qudel ⎰	$ 7.20 . . .	$200 "	$ 720 ——
	7	Gang Day ⎰ Billdeebe ⎱ Raceland ⎰	15.20	" " "	1,520 —— ——
	9	Quick Way ⎰ Oo Doo Doo ⎱ Hood Man ⎰	16.40	" " "	1,640 —— ——
				$1,600	$3,880 1,600
				NET GAIN	$2,280

(Work Sheet continued)

DATE	RACE	HORSE	WIN MUTUEL	WAGER	GROSS RETURN
2/3	1	Hudson Kid	$ ...	$200	$ ——
	2	Austin Venn	9.40	"	940
	4	Eternal Bim	3.80	"	380
	7	Sunaqua	...	"	——
	10	{Narcola	10.00	"	1,000
		{Liberty (ent.)	...	"	——
				$1,200	$2,320
					1,200
				NET GAIN	$1,120
2/5	1	{Big Hunk	$ ...	$200	$ ——
		{Cortilla	19.40	"	1,940
		{Eternal Broker	...	"	——
	2	Ticker Talk	7.40	"	740
	4	Ojo Rojo	5.00	"	500
	8	Curran'o	5.20	"	520
				$1,200	$3,700
					$1,200
				NET GAIN	$2,500
2/6	4	{Hood Man	$ ...	$200	$ ——
		{Ringthebell II	8.00	"	800
	9	{French Coat	7.60	"	760
		{Promenade	...	"	——
				$800	$1,560
					800
				NET GAIN	$ 760

(Work Sheet continued)

DATE	RACE	HORSE	WIN MUTUEL	WAGER	GROSS RETURN
2/7	1	Dis Sal	$ 4.60	$200	$ 460
	2	{ Jacquelin J.* } *tied*	. . .	"	——
		{ Lepus*	34.40	"	3,440
	3	Erin's Sister	45.20	"	4,520
	4	Marchaneta	. . .	"	——
	7	Count Tempus†	2.60	"	260
	9	{ Monteo	7.60	"	760
		{ Promenade	. . .	"	——
				$1,600	$9,440
					1,600
				NET GAIN	$7,840

* Speed-conversion control tie.
† Dead heat between Count Tempus and Royal Opening.

Our total net gain for the week—six racing days—was $18,700 at the Fair Grounds.

It will be noticed that when we had a dutching play, or tied speed-conversion contenders like Jacquelin J. and Lepus, we played the full unit on each, rather than split one unit among the two or three contenders. In many cases, as with Lepus, we get the best of the price, and therefore the maximum benefit from the dutching. However, this is no hard-and-fast rule. This is something for you to decide for yourself, according to your own circumstances, and will depend somewhat on how fast you want to amass a million dollars. If you decide to divide your 10 per cent of available capital equally among the two, or three, you are playing, there will still be a profit if one of them converts. And it's only one play among many you will make before you reach your goal.

If you are one of those who will have to start in a small way and build up to the suggested maximum of $200 flat per play, you can still get a quite good idea of how your operating bankroll will grow by using your own unit against the workout we have presented—or your own if you have already started your check-back—and increase your wagers (on paper) as the capital builds up. It should not take too long, even with a modest start, before you are in full swing.

I think we will all agree that that was a pretty fair week's work at Fair Grounds. We could go on and give the full month of New Orleans action, and profit, but we feel it will be more meaningful to check the other five tracks we have already worked with. It is our belief that to give such a cross section is much better and more reliable than to devote all the time, space, and energy to proving out further any one track. And you're going to check your own area tracks anyway, which will do you more good than if I gave you workouts of thousands of races. Chances are, you would look only at the total net gain.

Workouts are wonderful things if you make them yourself, for you pick up know-how and experience in that way that you can get in no other.

True, it is not experience under fire, but we all had to crawl before we could walk. And once you have gained facility at handling your control complex, you can devote all your concentration and effort to your actual play.

There is no denying that a difference does exist between making a paper check and playing for keeps at the track.

You are under no pressure while making mind-bets along with your paper check. A loss on paper takes nothing out of your pocket, but it might tend to shake your confidence in yourself and your control complex if you lost a large bet at the track.

This, I think, is the main reason you have heard fans complain that their system "worked fine on paper," but did not do well at the track. The pressure of actual operation caused them to deviate, probably without even realizing it.

For this reason, I consider a minimum thousand-race workout to be vital. By the time you have completed this much work with the complex, you will know what *you* can do as a selector. You will have established confidence in the system and in yourself as a selector. You will be less apt to deviate when the chips are down.

This is a thing you can and must do for yourself. All I can do for you is demonstrate the method, and try to let some of my confidence in it rub off on you. If I have accomplished this, then you will *want* to go ahead and prove it to yourself.

So, let's swing over to Florida and see how a week of operation at Hialeah compares with the week at the Fair Grounds.

CHAPTER FOURTEEN

Go Where the Money Is

Of the three winter tracks we have investigated, Hialeah is second in attendance and mutuel handle. On an average day at Hialeah, the attendance will go to about 17,000 and the mutuel handle on the fat side of one and a half million dollars. Fair Grounds, which we have just left, gets about one third the attendance and about one quarter as much handle. Santa Anita attendance runs somewhat over 20,000, but less than 25,000, on an average day (not a Saturday or holiday) and the mutuel handle will run close to two million dollars.

Someone once said that if you want to make money, go where the money is. The fact of the matter is, there is plenty of free-flowing money at all three of these tracks. The trick is in knowing how to make the Mutuel Monster disgorge.

DATE	RACE	HORSE	WIN MUTUEL	WAGER	GROSS RETURN
2/1		On the Quiet	$24.60	$200	$2,460
	1	Fausta	. . .	"	——
		Galan	. . .	"	——
	2	Foolish Question	16.40	"	1,640
	4	Grandpa David	5.10	"	510
	5	Gerald K	. . .	"	——

(Work Sheet continued)

DATE	RACE	HORSE	WIN MUTUEL	WAGER	GROSS RETURN
	7	Rideabout	...	"	——
		Three M. R.	10.40	"	1,040
		Linger On	6.30	"	630
	8	Iron Core	...	"	——
		Thunder Hill	...	"	——
	9	Bespoken	6.50	"	650
				$2,400	$6,930
					2,400
				NET GAIN	$4,530
2/2	2	Island Ford	$ 8.10	$200	$ 810
	4	Gutter Ball	...	"	——
	5	Lucky Viola	...	"	——
	6	Kisco Kid	76.00	"	7,600
	7	Miss J. G.	...	"	——
	9	Nutty Dream	...	"	——
		Blue Noor	...	"	——
		Route Sixty Six	9.60	"	960
				$1,600	$9,370
					1,600
				NET GAIN	$7,770
2/3	1	Bespoken	$14.00	$200	$1,400
	2	Aeropolis	...	"	——
		Alifan	...	"	——
	4	Come About	8.10	"	810
	7	Eurasia	9.40	"	940
	8	Refuting	10.40	"	1,040
				$1,200	$4,190
					1,200
				NET GAIN	$2,990

(*Work Sheet continued*)

DATE	RACE	HORSE	WIN MUTUEL	WAGER	GROSS RETURN
2/5		Seize Her	$ 8.00	$200	$ 800
	1	Misensation	. . .	"	————
		Sheer Delight	. . .	"	————
	5	Bay Liege	. . .	"	————
		Diderot	. . .	"	————
	7	Bronze Babu	13.50	"	1,350
	9	Motivation	. . .	"	————
		Nero	. . .	"	————
				$1,600	$2,150
					1,600
				NET GAIN	$ 550
2/6	5	Norther	$ 9.50	$200	$ 950
		Mr. Fantastic	. . .	"	————
	6	Running Free	5.50	"	550
	7	Portrayer	59.80	"	5,980
		Orazio	. . .	"	————
		Goodspeed	. . .	"	————
	8	Rideabout	. . .	"	————
		Three M. R.	5.00	"	500
				$1,600	$7,980
					1,600
				NET GAIN	$6,380
2/7	2	Manor Hill	$38.60	$200	$3,860
		Poet's Eye	. . .	"	————
	4	Just Bully	3.20	"	320
	5	Moss Eater	. . .	"	————
	6	Cicada	3.50	"	350
	9	Great Dome	7.20	"	720
				$1,200	$5,250
					1,200
				NET GAIN	$4,050

So the Mutuel Monster at Hialeah coughed up a nice total of $26,270 net. This for the first six days of racing in February, 1962, and another solid reason why I am a bit partial to the Florida winter racing season.

Which reminds me of a chap I got to know real well around the California winter racing plants back some years ago when we lived in California.

This man, and his wife, were from New Jersey, so you would naturally expect them to trek south to Florida when the cold winds hit the northeast, especially since the lady owned a horse who was running in Florida at the time.

The reason why they came to California instead? The difference in "take" in the two states. In Florida, it's a 15 per cent bite. In California, only 13 per cent. So, for a 2 per cent difference, they traveled all the way to California. The amusing part of this is, the man was dead serious about it—and yet he was a man who never had a winning year. Since a loser never pays any part of the track "take," what possible weight did it carry in his operation? But they were nice friendly folks and we were always glad to see them appear for the California merry-go-round.

Frankly, the "take" have never worried me one bit. It has to be paid, just like income and other taxes, but I've never heard anybody claim that you can't win at the game of life because of the 20 per cent (and up) income tax "take." It seems to me it's a question of very simple mathematics. If you make enough to get along in a comfortable fashion, whether in salary or race track profits, the "take," whatever it is, is only a minor irritation. Beefing about it serves little purpose except as a conversation piece.

So let's journey out to California, to Santa Anita, and make

our comparison, moneywise—keeping in mind that at Santa
Anita we have a five-day racing week.

DATE	RACE	HORSE	WIN MUTUEL	WAGER	GROSS RETURN
2/1	1	City Babe	$13.20	$200	$1,320
	4	Byk	. . .	"	————
	5	Bride of Egypt	5.60	"	560
	6	⎰Gun Box	9.20	"	920
		⎰Daiichi	. . .	"	————
		⎱Sweet Lilly	. . .	"	
	7	Art Market	16.40	"	1,640
				$1,400	$4,440
					1,400
				NET GAIN	$3,040

DATE	RACE	HORSE	WIN MUTUEL	WAGER	GROSS RETURN
2/2	1	Go Sue Go	$ 3.20	$200	$ 320
	2	⎰One Day	. . .	"	————
		⎱I'm High	23.60	"	2,360
	5	Pixie Erin (ent.)	4.60	"	460
	6	Windy Sea	3.40	"	340
				$1,000	$3,480
					1,000
				NET GAIN	$2,480

DATE	RACE	HORSE	WIN MUTUEL	WAGER	GROSS RETURN
2/3	1	Indian Village	$ . . .	$200	$——
	2	Rancho Day	28.60	"	2,860
	4	Atalyero	. . .	"	————
	5	Park Royal	8.80	"	880
				$800	$3,740
					800
				NET GAIN	$2,940

(*Work Sheet continued*)

DATE	RACE	HORSE	WIN MUTUEL	WAGER	GROSS RETURN
2/6	1	Wingmaster	$ ...	$200	$ ——
	4	Sweet CeeCee	...	"	——
	6	Sue III	8.80	"	880
	7	Bright Holly	3.20	"	320
				$800	$1,200
					800
				NET GAIN	$ 400
2/7	1	{ Leaning Tower	$ ...	$200	$ ——
		{ Ardeb	8.60	"	860
	4	{ Stellina	...	"	——
		{ Jet Parade	...	"	——
		{ Kea	31.20	"	3,120
				$1,000	$3,980
					1,000
				NET GAIN	$2,980

So we journeyed way out yonder where the money is, and picked up $11,840 for the five-day week.

We now have a pretty good cross section of winter racing—three full weeks at three widely separated locales. Are you beginning to have confidence, as we hope you are, that our control complex will make money anywhere?—and the kind of money you're interested in, or you wouldn't have picked up this book?

Now let's head back East for some spring racing. We'll stop in Maryland first, okay?

CHAPTER FIFTEEN

Laurel Park Revisited

Since we now face Laurel with less trepidation after seeing what we could accomplish there through dutching and letting the bars down a bit, we can hope for a good week of action and profits.

It occurs to us, at this point, especially in view of the amount of dutching required, and hence larger investments, that some of you fans, particularly those of you who have been in the habit of playing the minimum, or perhaps five-dollar play, will be uneasy about playing the larger amounts.

Look at it this way. If a play is not worth risking our suggested maximum, providing the proper amount of operating capital is available, then it is not worth risking the minimum two dollars. Relatively speaking, there is no difference between a two-dollar play, or a two-hundred-dollar one. Each should be no more than 10 per cent of available capital. Or, if you are naturally more conservative-minded, make your unit 5 per cent. It makes not the slightest difference to me. It just takes a bit longer to get where you're going.

The point I'm trying to make is this: If you ever find yourself saying, "I might risk a lesser bet on this one, but not the full treatment," you'd better back off and pass the race. If, in your opinion, the selection will not stand the full backing, neither is it worth a two-buck play. There is something wrong. You are thinking of *gambling* a minimum amount instead of *invest*ing in the full control play. This should be a warning signal. Either you have sloughed your work, or are letting your emotions take charge of your thinking.

Rework the race, objectively, and if it still is not worth the full treatment in your opinion, then it is not worth a play at all. Not even on paper, for what you are doing in your paper check should form the habits you will later bring to actual operation.

It is true—and I'm sure you noticed it—that while we were engaged in the long play-by-play work that has brought us to this point, I occasionally stole a long lead off base. These may have seemed to you to have involved certain risks, but they were calculated ones. I was still convinced that I had the percentages with me.

For instance, when we failed to get any action at all with our speed-conversion control on the first go-round at Laurel, and I had to fudge a bit to get Cross Up and Sunaqua, (in the second go-round using class-condition), these two were still the only logical probabilities in their respective races *under the circumstances*—the circumstances being that this was a brand new spring meeting with insufficient line to make normal selections. But by fudging a little—though not beyond limits we had already studied—these were still the most likely winners when compared with the others.

You, too, will eventually reach the point where these calculated risks become recognizable. As you work your complete control complex from race to race, more and more you will see the complete picture. Even when you are working only with speed-conversion control, in the first four races, you will notice the other things we have studied, and will be influenced by them—safely influenced, I should say. Or when you are working the class-condition, you may possibly notice some especially fast time, or one of the three speed horses we have already worked, which might now be used to make a class distinction. Or you may see that a selection you have already listed as playable, might be combined to better advantage in a dutching play.

I do not wish to rush you on this. The whole picture will gradually emerge for you as you continue with your thousand-race paper work. Don't try to force it. It will come of its own volition.

Now let's look at a week's work at Laurel.

DATE	RACE	HORSE	WIN MUTUEL	WAGER	GROSS RETURN
4/2	2	Debate	$ 8.40	$200	$ 840
		Miss Houston	. . .	"	——
	4	Cross Up	18.00	"	1,800
		Pomp's Favorite	. . .	"	——
	5	San Sebastion	20.80	"	2,080
		Entourage	. . .	"	——
	9	Sunaqua	7.80	"	780
				$1,400	$ 5,500
					1,400
				NET GAIN	$ 4,100
4/3	1	Pentonian	$ . . .	$200	$ ——
	4	Bill Huey	. . .	"	——
	6	Coach and Four	4.80	"	480

(Work Sheet continued)

DATE	RACE	HORSE	WIN MUTUEL	WAGER	GROSS RETURN
	8	Crackpot	12.80	"	1,280
	9	Skilligolee	...	"	——
		County Agent	35.00	"	3,500
				$1,200	$ 5,260
					1,200
				NET GAIN	$ 4,060
4/4	1	Bay Drive	$ ...	$200	$ ——
	4	Running Boy	...	"	——
		Ring Shot	...	"	——
		Pine Scout	63.80	"	6,380
	5	Cumula	12.20	"	1,220
	7	Best Brother	...	"	——
		Polarity	...	"	——
		Invigor	39.40	"	3,940
	9	Daytime Bully	...	"	——
				$1,800	$11,540
					1,800
				NET GAIN	$ 9,740
4/5	1	Extra Margin	$12.00	$200	$ 1,200
		King Midas	...	"	——
		Robdix	...	"	——
	2	Penshoe	...	"	——
	6	Equimiss	8.80	"	880
		Dolly's Moment	...	"	——
				$1,200	$ 2,080
					1,200
				NET GAIN	$ 880

(*Work Sheet continued*)

DATE	RACE	HORSE	WIN MUTUEL	WAGER	GROSS RETURN
4/6		Behead	$ ...	$200	$ ——
	2	Fondness	...	"	——
		Waltzing Harp	24.00	"	2,400
				$600	$ 2,400
					600
				NET GAIN	$ 1,800
4/7	2	Hampo	$ 8.80	$200	$ 880
	4	Iris H.	...	"	——
	6	Adorette	6.20	"	620
	7	Hot Cargo	4.20	"	420
	9	Desert Goddess	28.00	"	2,800
		Winter League	...	"	——
				$1,200	$ 4,720
					1,200
				NET GAIN	$ 3,520

So, we have a sort of surprise at Laurel, a total net gain of $24,100 for the six racing days in the first week of April. And since this meeting opened on March 31, 1962, we practically got in there at first blood.

Now, in case any of you are sweating over how I qualified Crackpot in the 8th race on April 3, I'm afraid I must plead guilty of a small whizzer here. This horse I qualified on stakes class, since it was clearly stated at the bottom of his past performances that he had been nominated for the Kentucky Derby, the Preakness, and the Belmont Stakes. So with this amount of class edge, and with the Derby only a month away, the horse was obviously dropped into a soft spot in preparation for the "run for the roses."

Just another reason for keeping your eyes open when scanning the record of each and every contestant.

Here's another little wrinkle that may prove helpful from time to time. You will recall that we used speed-standard ratings to determine if a horse won that last race in slower time than he was capable of? Well, we can make use of a ratings comparison of the last race over the previous, too, if needed or desired. For instance, a horse that won his previous race in slower time than he was capable of, then came back to run second, thus setting up a negative (visual) 1/p, might well cause us to wonder. By a ratings comparison, we might find that that race was actually faster than the previous one, in which he won. By ratings, then, the 1/p becomes positive, whereas the visual 1/p was negative. If the horse, say, had a very strong closing pattern in that last race, which caused your suspicion about the visual negative 1/p, the standards 1/p has now cleared up the mystery for you. This beastie could now be seriously considered as an ultimate selection.

So—on to Aqueduct.

DATE	RACE	HORSE	WIN MUTUEL	WAGER	GROSS RETURN
4/2	2	Miney Myerson	$ 9.00	$200	$ 900
	6	Shiny Button	14.30	"	1,430
	8	Barracho J. J.	4.10	"	410
	9	Solar Flare	...	"	—
				$800	$2,740
					800
				Net Gain	$1,940

(*Work Sheet continued*)

DATE	RACE	HORSE	WIN MUTUEL	WAGER	GROSS RETURN
4/3	2	Sandy Fork	$ . . .	$200	$ ——
	4	Gaza Stripper	9.10	"	910
	5	Surfer	9.40	"	940
		Grey Ghost	. . .	"	
	6	Scan the Sky	19.40	"	1,940
		Hildy's Lou	. . .	"	——
		Ocala Breeze	. . .	"	
	8	Merry New Year	5.00	"	500
	9	Heavenly Girl	. . .	"	——
		Broker's Lass	6.60	"	660
				$2,000	$4,950
					2,000
				NET GAIN	$2,950
4/4	2	Miss Stonie	$ . . .	$200	$ ——
		Dorothy Buck	. . .	"	——
		Penny Circle	66.70	"	6,670
	4	Gemormont	. . .	"	——
		Madame Bob	. . .	"	
	5	Oscar Award	6.30	"	630
		Dark Legacy	. . .	"	——
		Nutty Dream	. . .	"	
	8	Fauve	7.10	"	710
				$1,800	$8,010
					1,800
				NET GAIN	$6,210
4/5	4	Brass Knuckles	$10.90	$200	$1,090
	5	Hold the Fort	7.50	"	750
				$400	$1,840
					400
				NET GAIN	$1,440

(*Work Sheet continued*)

DATE	RACE	HORSE	WIN MUTUEL	WAGER	GROSS RETURN
4/6	1	Gay Empress	$ ...	$200	$ ——
	2	Prophet's Call	41.90	"	4,190
		⎰Cape Canaveral	...	"	——
	3	⎱Senrac S.	...	"	
		⎰Mad Fury	39.90	"	3,990
	4	Dotty Kirsten	9.40	"	940
	6	Garwol	4.40	"	440
				$1,400	$9,560
					1,400
				NET GAIN	$8,160

Our net gain for the six-day week at Aqueduct was $20,700. This, of course, is another of those tracks where the money is, but it was nowhere near as "hard pickings" as Santa Anita, where we made a good deal less. And so it goes. Santa Anita should not stay at the bottom of the profit list as the rest of the meeting unfolds.

Going into the final week of our six-week cross-section workout, it is hoped that each of you has followed the process with *Forms* or *Telegraphs* open before you, and that you have already acquired enough of these to make *your* thousand-race workout.

And so to Florida—and Gulfstream Park.

DATE	RACE	HORSE	WIN MUTUEL	WAGER	GROSS RETURN
4/2	1	El Misterio	$ 6.50	$200	$ 650
	2	Star Piper	6.80	"	680
		⎰Trimette	14.80	"	1,480
	3	⎱Harriet's Comet	...	"	——

(*Work Sheet continued*)

DATE	RACE	HORSE	WIN MUTUEL	WAGER	GROSS RETURN
	4	Absconder	14.20	"	1,420
	5	Brave Spartan	3.90	"	390
	6	Roster	. . .	"	——
	8	Count Rose	. . .	"	——
				$1,600	$ 4,620
					1,600
				NET GAIN	$ 3,020
4/3	1	Sun-Sun Corda	$ 8.00	$200	$ 800
	4	Madre	. . .	"	——
	7	Sky Bid	13.10	"	1,310
	8	Gail's Guy	. . .	"	——
		Shine Sun	6.50	"	650
	9	Strong Wind	46.00	"	4,600
		Big Steve	. . .	"	——
				$1,400	$ 7,360
					1,400
				NET GAIN	$ 5,960
4/4	1	Sir Charmain	$ . . .	$200	$ ——
	2	Weeper Lea	9.50	"	950
	3	Artist Town	. . .	"	——
		Sirezzal	. . .	"	——
		Sol Invictus	18.40	"	1,840
	4	Trusting Faith	16.70	"	1,670
		Misdirected	. . .	"	——
	5	Pa Pitt	27.00	"	2,700
	6	Vengativo	13.20	"	1,320
		Fiery Cadet	. . .	"	——

	8	{ Caricature	. . .	"	——
		{ Stacked Up	56.30	"	5,630
				$2,400	$14,110
					2,400
				NET GAIN	$11,710
4/5	2	Air Delight	$11.90	$200	$ 1,190
	4	Fifth Filly	. . .	"	——
	5	Rededication	7.90	"	790
	7	Show Tune	7.50	"	750
	8	Flavio	. . .	"	——
				$1,000	$ 2,730
					1,000
				NET GAIN	$ 1,730
4/6	4	In Between	$ . . .	$200	$ ——
	5	Summer Savory	3.20	"	320
	7	His Legend	7.20	"	720
	8	Prim Flower	. . .	"	——
		{ Volborg	22.80	"	2,280
	9	{ Quiet Brook	. . .	"	——
		{ Magician II	. . .	"	——
				$1,400	$ 3,320
					1,400
				NET GAIN	$ 1,920
4/7	1	Little Nita	$ . . .	$200	$ ——
	2	{ Barely Nothing	17.70	"	1,770
		{ Delnita II	. . .	"	——
	3	Cosmic Trend	14.40	"	1,440
	4	{ Raven Wing	6.30	"	630
		{ False Alarm	. . .	"	——
		{ Legend Dancer	. . .	"	——
	6	{ Big Music	9.30	"	930
		{ Diploma	. . .	"	——

7	Aeroflint	...	"	———
9	{ Lady Susan	22.70	"	2,270
	{ Fire Call	...	"	———

| | $2,400 | $ 7,040 |
| | | 2,400 |

NET GAIN $ 4,640

This adds up to a net gain of $28,980.00 for the six-day racing week at Gulfstream Park.

CHAPTER SIXTEEN *The Pudding*

Before we leave you to your labors, we are now in a position—a good position, we think—to give you the final answers to your question about how this all adds up to a million dollars, and over what period of time.

The total net gain for our six-week cross-section amounts to $131,370. This reduced to a mean average of $21,895 per week.

Now, assuming this is a correct average for your action at whatever tracks you choose to patronize, and assuming you intend to persevere from one operation to another for a full-time effort, or fifty-two weeks in the year——

Taking the above $21,895 weekly average and multiplying it by 52 weeks, we get $1,138,540.

You're on your own now, so get to work—and it *is* work. I didn't promise you anything easy. The only easy way to get a million is to inherit it. For those of us who don't have a rich uncle, there is no *easy* way.

A professional cynic once said there is no *honest* way to make a million dollars. Obviously, he did not know about our control complex.

A PERSONAL WORD FROM MELVIN POWERS
PUBLISHER, WILSHIRE BOOK COMPANY

Dear Friend:

My goal is to publish interesting, informative, and inspirational books. You can help me accomplish this by answering the following questions, either by phone or by mail. Or, if convenient for you, I would welcome the opportunity to visit with you in my office and hear your comments in person.

Did you enjoy reading this book? Why?

Would you enjoy reading another similar book?

What idea in the book impressed you the most?

If applicable to your situation, have you incorporated this idea in your daily life?

Is there a chapter that could serve as a theme for an entire book? Please explain.

If you have an idea for a book, I would welcome discussing it with you. If you already have one in progress, write or call me concerning possible publication. I can be reached at (213) 875-1711 or (213) 983-1105.

Sincerely yours,

MELVIN POWERS

12015 Sherman Road
North Hollywood, California 91605

MELVIN POWERS SELF-IMPROVEMENT LIBRARY

ASTROLOGY

BRIDGE

BUSINESS, STUDY & REFERENCE

CALLIGRAPHY

CHESS & CHECKERS

COOKERY & HERBS

HEALING POWER OF HERBS *May Bethel*		3.00
HERB HANDBOOK *Dawn MacLeod*		2.00
HERBS FOR COOKING AND HEALING *Dr. Donald Law*		2.00
HERBS FOR HEALTH—How to Grow & Use Them *Louise Evans Doole*		2.00
HOME GARDEN COOKBOOK—Delicious Natural Food Recipes *Ken Kraft*		3.00
MEDICAL HERBALIST *edited by Dr. J. R. Yemm*		3.00
NATURAL FOOD COOKBOOK *Dr. Harry C. Bond*		3.00
NATURE'S MEDICINES *Richard Lucas*		3.00
VEGETABLE GARDENING FOR BEGINNERS *Hugh Wiberg*		2.00
VEGETABLES FOR TODAY'S GARDENS *R. Milton Carleton*		2.00
VEGETARIAN COOKERY *Janet Walker*		3.00
VEGETARIAN COOKING MADE EASY & DELECTABLE *Veronica Vezza*		2.00
VEGETARIAN DELIGHTS—A Happy Cookbook for Health *K. R. Mehta*		2.00
VEGETARIAN GOURMET COOKBOOK *Joyce McKinnel*		2.00

GAMBLING & POKER

ADVANCED POKER STRATEGY & WINNING PLAY *A. D. Livingston*		3.00
HOW NOT TO LOSE AT POKER *Jeffrey Lloyd Castle*		3.00
HOW TO WIN AT DICE GAMES *Skip Frey*		3.00
HOW TO WIN AT POKER *Terence Reese & Anthony T. Watkins*		2.00
SECRETS OF WINNING POKER *George S. Coffin*		3.00
WINNING AT CRAPS *Dr. Lloyd T. Commins*		2.00
WINNING AT GIN *Chester Wander & Cy Rice*		3.00
WINNING AT 21—An Expert's Guide *John Archer*		3.00
WINNING POKER SYSTEMS *Norman Zadeh*		3.00

HEALTH

DR. LINDNER'S SPECIAL WEIGHT CONTROL METHOD		1.50
HELP YOURSELF TO BETTER SIGHT *Margaret Darst Corbett*		3.00
HOW TO IMPROVE YOUR VISION *Dr. Robert A. Kraskin*		2.00
HOW YOU CAN STOP SMOKING PERMANENTLY *Ernest Caldwell*		2.00
MIND OVER PLATTER *Peter G. Lindner, M.D.*		2.00
NATURE'S WAY TO NUTRITION & VIBRANT HEALTH *Robert J. Scrutton*		3.00
NEW CARBOHYDRATE DIET COUNTER *Patti Lopez-Pereira*		1.50
PSYCHEDELIC ECSTASY *William Marshall & Gilbert W. Taylor*		2.00
REFLEXOLOGY *Dr. Maybelle Segal*		2.00
YOU CAN LEARN TO RELAX *Dr. Samuel Gutwirth*		2.00
YOUR ALLERGY—What To Do About It *Allan Knight, M.D.*		2.00

HOBBIES

BATON TWIRLING—A Complete Illustrated Guide *Doris Wheelus*		4.00
BEACHCOMBING FOR BEGINNERS *Norman Hickin*		2.00
BLACKSTONE'S MODERN CARD TRICKS *Harry Blackstone*		2.00
BLACKSTONE'S SECRETS OF MAGIC *Harry Blackstone*		2.00
BUTTERFLIES		2.50
COIN COLLECTING FOR BEGINNERS *Burton Hobson & Fred Reinfeld*		2.00
ENTERTAINING WITH ESP *Tony 'Doc' Shiels*		2.00
400 FASCINATING MAGIC TRICKS YOU CAN DO *Howard Thurston*		3.00
GOULD'S GOLD & SILVER GUIDE TO COINS *Maurice Gould*		2.00
HOW I TURN JUNK INTO FUN AND PROFIT *Sari*		3.00
HOW TO PLAY THE HARMONICA FOR FUN AND PROFIT *Hal Leighton*		3.00
HOW TO WRITE A HIT SONG & SELL IT *Tommy Boyce*		7.00
JUGGLING MADE EASY *Rudolf Dittrich*		2.00
MAGIC MADE EASY *Byron Wels*		2.00
SEW SIMPLY, SEW RIGHT *Mini Rhea & F. Leighton*		2.00
STAMP COLLECTING FOR BEGINNERS *Burton Hobson*		2.00
STAMP COLLECTING FOR FUN & PROFIT *Frank Cetin*		2.00

HORSE PLAYERS' WINNING GUIDES

BETTING HORSES TO WIN *Les Conklin*		3.00
ELIMINATE THE LOSERS *Bob McKnight*		3.00
HOW TO PICK WINNING HORSES *Bob McKnight*		3.00
HOW TO WIN AT THE RACES *Sam (The Genius) Lewin*		3.00
HOW YOU CAN BEAT THE RACES *Jack Kavanagh*		3.00

_____SEXUALLY ADEQUATE MALE *Frank S. Caprio, M.D.*   3.00

METAPHYSICS & OCCULT

_____BOOK OF TALISMANS, AMULETS & ZODIACAL GEMS *William Pavitt*   4.00
_____CONCENTRATION—A Guide to Mental Mastery *Mouni Sadhu*   3.00
_____CRITIQUES OF GOD *Edited by Peter Angeles*   7.00
_____DREAMS & OMENS REVEALED *Fred Gettings*   2.00
_____EXTRASENSORY PERCEPTION *Simeon Edmunds*   2.00
_____EXTRA-TERRESTRIAL INTELLIGENCE—The First Encounter   6.00
_____FORTUNE TELLING WITH CARDS *P. Foli*   2.00
_____HANDWRITING ANALYSIS MADE EASY *John Marley*   2.00
_____HANDWRITING TELLS *Nadya Olyanova*   3.00
_____HOW TO UNDERSTAND YOUR DREAMS *Geoffrey A. Dudley*   2.00
_____ILLUSTRATED YOGA *William Zorn*   3.00
_____IN DAYS OF GREAT PEACE *Mouni Sadhu*   3.00
_____KING SOLOMON'S TEMPLE IN THE MASONIC TRADITION *Alex Horne*   5.00
_____LSD—THE AGE OF MIND *Bernard Roseman*   2.00
_____MAGICIAN—His training and work *W. E. Butler*   2.00
_____MEDITATION *Mouni Sadhu*   4.00
_____MODERN NUMEROLOGY *Morris C. Goodman*   3.00
_____NUMEROLOGY—ITS FACTS AND SECRETS *Ariel Yvon Taylor*   2.00
_____PALMISTRY MADE EASY *Fred Gettings*   2.00
_____PALMISTRY MADE PRACTICAL *Elizabeth Daniels Squire*   3.00
_____PALMISTRY SECRETS REVEALED *Henry Frith*   2.00
_____PRACTICAL YOGA *Ernest Wood*   3.00
_____PROPHECY IN OUR TIME *Martin Ebon*   2.50
_____PSYCHOLOGY OF HANDWRITING *Nadya Olyanova*   3.00
_____SEEING INTO THE FUTURE *Harvey Day*   2.00
_____SUPERSTITION—Are you superstitious? *Eric Maple*   2.00
_____TAROT *Mouni Sadhu*   4.00
_____TAROT OF THE BOHEMIANS *Papus*   5.00
_____TEST YOUR ESP *Martin Ebon*   2.00
_____WAYS TO SELF-REALIZATION *Mouni Sadhu*   3.00
_____WITCHCRAFT, MAGIC & OCCULTISM—A Fascinating History *W. B. Crow*   3.00
_____WITCHCRAFT—THE SIXTH SENSE *Justine Glass*   2.00
_____WORLD OF PSYCHIC RESEARCH *Hereward Carrington*   2.00
_____YOU CAN ANALYZE HANDWRITING *Robert Holder*   2.00

SELF-HELP & INSPIRATIONAL

_____CYBERNETICS WITHIN US *Y. Saparina*   3.00
_____DAILY POWER FOR JOYFUL LIVING *Dr. Donald Curtis*   2.00
_____DOCTOR PSYCHO-CYBERNETICS *Maxwell Maltz, M.D.*   3.00
_____DYNAMIC THINKING *Melvin Powers*   2.00
_____EXUBERANCE—Your Guide to Happiness & Fulfillment *Dr. Paul Kurtz*   3.00
_____GREATEST POWER IN THE UNIVERSE *U. S. Andersen*   4.00
_____GROW RICH WHILE YOU SLEEP *Ben Sweetland*   3.00
_____GROWTH THROUGH REASON *Albert Ellis, Ph.D.*   3.00
_____GUIDE TO DEVELOPING YOUR POTENTIAL *Herbert A. Otto, Ph.D.*   3.00
_____GUIDE TO LIVING IN BALANCE *Frank S. Caprio, M.D.*   2.00
_____HELPING YOURSELF WITH APPLIED PSYCHOLOGY *R. Henderson*   2.00
_____HELPING YOURSELF WITH PSYCHIATRY *Frank S. Caprio, M.D.*   2.00
_____HOW TO ATTRACT GOOD LUCK *A. H. Z. Carr*   3.00
_____HOW TO CONTROL YOUR DESTINY *Norvell*   2.00
_____HOW TO DEVELOP A WINNING PERSONALITY *Martin Panzer*   3.00
_____HOW TO DEVELOP AN EXCEPTIONAL MEMORY *Young & Gibson*   3.00
_____HOW TO OVERCOME YOUR FEARS *M. P. Leahy, M.D.*   2.00
_____HOW YOU CAN HAVE CONFIDENCE AND POWER *Les Giblin*   3.00
_____HUMAN PROBLEMS & HOW TO SOLVE THEM *Dr. Donald Curtis*   3.00
_____I CAN *Ben Sweetland*   4.00
_____I WILL *Ben Sweetland*   3.00
_____LEFT-HANDED PEOPLE *Michael Barsley*   3.00
_____MAGIC IN YOUR MIND *U. S. Andersen*   3.00

The books listed above can be obtained from your book dealer or directly from Melvin Powers. When ordering, please remit 25c per book postage & handling. Send for our free illustrated catalog of self-improvement books.

Melvin Powers

12015 Sherman Road, No. Hollywood, California 91605